Understanding Semantics-Based Decision Support

Understanding Semantics-Based Decision Support

Sarika Jain

CRC Press
Taylor & Francis Group
Boca Raton London New York

CRC Press is an imprint of the
Taylor & Francis Group, an **informa** business

A CHAPMAN & HALL BOOK

First edition published 2020
by CRC Press
6000 Broken Sound Parkway NW, Suite 300, Boca Raton, FL 33487-2742

and by CRC Press
2 Park Square, Milton Park, Abingdon, Oxon, OX14 4RN

© 2021 Taylor & Francis Group, LLC

CRC Press is an imprint of Taylor & Francis Group, LLC

Library of Congress Cataloging-in-Publication Data

Library of Congress Control Number: 2020946041

ISBN: 978-0-367-44313-9 (hbk)
ISBN: 978-1-003-00892-7 (ebk)

Typeset in Palatino
by MPS Limited, Dehradun

Table of Contents

Foreword

UNIVERSITY *of* MARYLAND
EASTERN SHORE
DIVISION *of* ACADEMIC AFFAIRS
School of Business and Technology
Department of Mathematics and Computer Science

EASC, 2105   Office: 410-651-6426
Princess Anne, Maryland 21853   Fax: 410-651-7673

Foreword Note for "Understanding Semantics-Based Decision Support"

One of the main features of the semantic web is that it provides a framework for understanding the processing of information and its associated troubleshooting issues, thereby creating easy communication for data sharing among machines.

Web technologies have gone through significant changes during the last few years, using different technologies like Artificial Intelligence (AI), the semantic web, decision support systems, and more. One of the objectives of this integrated approach has been to provide communication between machines for data sharing. Web technology offers interaction between users, whereas semantic web technology allows an understanding of information processing and the interpretation of data. AI technology provides a mapping between users and computers so that they can be used by each other for data sharing. Various components needed in web technologies for data sharing, like the design of scripts and programs, and the design and use of tags, are supported by extensible markup language (XML). This language supports a framework known as Resource Description Framework (RDF) that decodes the meanings of these components and formats and their relationships so that users can easily visualize it all. Another framework, which provides stronger machine interpretability than RDF, is Web Ontology Language (OWL). It is built on top of RDF but has its own vocabulary and stronger syntax. A query language known as SPARQL Protocol and RDF Query Language (SPARQL) supports applications for RDF data and extraction from traditional databases, relational databases, XML, HTML, and more.

In semantic web technology, one of the main issues researchers are dealing with is the accurate interpretation and manipulation of relationships. Inference has been incorporated into these developments for accurate data integration and handling of data inconsistencies on the web, but complete re-annotation of the web still seems to be a complex challenge for future web design. In the meantime, we have seen a different approach of understanding web formats: software agents (a very popular approach used in handling load-balancing problems in heterogeneous distributed computing) have been introduced not for machine understandability of web pages but for information retrieval and natural-language processing. Natural-language processing/programming (NLP) is based on AI and linguistics and provides easy interaction between machines and human (natural) language. The World Wide Web Consortium (W3C) has introduced a number of standards for semantic web decision support technologies like RDF, OWL, and SPARQL.

Semantic web technologies and decision support systems have been used in the last decade to provide accurate solutions for a number of applications like information integration and sharing, web-service annotation and discovery, retrieval and knowledge management, intelligent business strategies, social networking and collaboration systems, emergency response management, healthcare systems, and many more.

Some commercial products are available, including IBM Decision Optimization for Watson Studio, IBM SPSS Predictive Analytics Enterprise, LogicNets, Analytica Optimizer (Lumina Decision Systems), and others.

Decision support systems are already taught in multiple courses. With the semantic web and the usage of semantic technologies being added to the curricula of universities for graduate and master's courses, this is the right time to bring such a book to market. I am pleased to introduce this book, *Understanding Semantic-Based Decision Support*, which is at the intersection of sematic technologies and decision support.

The uniqueness of the book is evident from the fact that the author is trying to build the concepts of decision support and AI into semantic web technology. This new integration of technologies will be a building block for future web designs for machines to perform data exchanges, processing, storage, retrieval, and management. This book is unique and a must-read in various aspects:

- Gives an in-depth treatment of various basic components needed for future semantic web decision support systems.
- Describes the power of ontologies for better data management.
- Provides an overview of knowledge engineering, including ontology engineering, tools, and techniques.
- Provides sample development procedures for creating domain ontologies.
- Depicts the utility of ontological representation in situation awareness.

- Demonstrates a recommendation engine for unconventional emergencies using a hybrid reasoning approach.
- Explains the hybrid reasoning approach, utilizing case-based and rule-based reasoning, in great detail.
- Explains how to make better utilization of resources when an emergency strikes.

The utility of semantic technologies for unconventional emergencies is depicted in the book, along with different use cases. Research-oriented readers can take this work to next level, as various future directions are presented as closing remarks.

I am confident that students and practitioners will find this book very useful for learning and practicing on future web technologies.

Best regards,

Gurdeep S Hura

Gurdeep S. Hura, PhD
Professor of Computer Science
Department of Mathematics and Computer Science,
University of Maryland Eastern Shore, Princess Anne, MD 21853
gshura@umes.edu, 410-651-6426

Preface

Since 2008, I have worked in the field of knowledge representation in Artificial Intelligence, specifically in knowledge-based systems for the last five to six years. This book is an attempt to establish for readers the importance of using semantic data models by creating interoperable data stores and thereby enhancing situation awareness and decision support. It provides an introduction to knowledge-based systems and knowledge engineering to experts from all domains. It covers extracts from a few postgraduate project dissertations I have supervised and one funded research project.

Due to many technological trends—including the internet of things, cloud computing, and smart devices—huge data is generated daily and at unprecedented rates. The volume of data worldwide grows 50 times year over year. The so-called three Vs—volume (exabytes, petabytes), variety (heterogeneity), and velocity (millions of transactions per second)—pose numerous challenges in the storage and processing of this huge data. We need to make this data an enabler in achieving competitive advantage. Traditional data techniques and platforms are not efficient, because of issues concerning responsiveness, flexibility, performance, uncertainty, heterogeneity, scalability, accuracy, and more. To manage these huge data sets and store archives for longer periods, we need granular access to massively evolving data sets. Addressing this gap has been an important and well-recognized interdisciplinary area of computer science. There is a growing need for metadata and semantics in every real-life application under any domain, whether it be sensor networks, cognitive sciences, human-computer interaction, or anything else. In particular, developing intelligent applications to provide resource-management assistance and situation awareness in order to fetch real-time recommendations and decision support is the application of interest for this book.

Emergency response decisions demand extraordinary efforts because of the fundamental challenges involved. The requirement is to prepare the people, the government, and all the stakeholders to handle catastrophic disasters. Semantic web technologies have been found the most important ingredient in building artificially intelligent knowledge-based systems, as they aid machines in integrating and processing resources contextually and intelligently. The industry is rapidly innovating various products and services for the web of data based on the technologies and standards given by the W3C.

This work is an attempt to integrate the full potential of existing approaches, tools, techniques, and methodologies to provide situation awareness and advisory support to end-users in a seamless manner.

Ontologies describe the meaning (i.e., the semantics) of content in a way that can be interpreted by machines. This book presents the prototypical development of a knowledge-driven situation awareness and advisory support that provides real-time information in order to provide intelligent decision support. Technologies standardized by the W3C have been utilized for representing, storing, querying, evaluating, and further enriching knowledge.

Key Features

This book is unique in several respects:

- As a reference book/monograph, it is the first of its kind to discuss what is going on in knowledge-based systems research in an easy-to-understand manner for non-experts in computer science. Specifically, chapter 2 provides a review of the practices and reasoning of ontological engineering.

- Graduate and undergraduate students doing courses in Artificial Intelligence, the semantic web, knowledge engineering, and decision support systems can benefit from this text. Even those pursuing courses in management and decision support can understand how to create working prototypes.

- After reading the book, a novice in the field of computer science can get a hands-on lesson in how to utilize semantic web technologies for real-world problems. A case study on unconventional emergencies is presented in the book with two sample emergencies, one natural and the other artificial.

- The principal benefit of the book is to bring forward the idea of applying semantic web technologies on a sample application domain, with the aim of bringing together the technology and the domain into a single digestible narrative suitable for busy readers who are not experts in statistics or computer science.

This book will be useful for various categories of users:

- senior undergraduate and graduate students
- academics and researchers
- practitioners in all application domains

There have been a number of books with "decision support," "situation awareness," and "semantic web" in their titles separately, but no single book covers all these aspects at once. As the semantic web and its applications are entering the newest curricula at educational institutions worldwide, with not many pertinent books available, it is high time to introduce such a book that can serve as a text or reference.

Quick Guide to Reading the Book

An effort has been made to keep all the chapters as independent as possible. The following breakdown provides a reading guide to the flow of material in the book, briefly sketching any dependencies between the chapters. It is advisable to go through at least the abstracts of the chapters you are skipping.

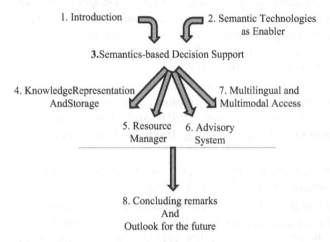

The book is organized as follows:

- The first chapter sets the pace of reading the book by presenting motivating scenarios for combining semantic technologies and decision support, including a running example. It is an introductory chapter that presents the wider context and significance of the book.

- The second chapter introduces the relevant foundations of semantic technologies, including Resource Description Framework (RDF) and Web Ontology Language (OWL), standard reasoning services, and technologies for storing and querying semantic data. This chapter explains in sufficient detail all these enabling technologies. This chapter can be skipped by general readers who are not interested in the various semantic tools and methodologies available.

- Chapter 3 advocates the requirement of a semantics-enabled decision support system for situation awareness that can provide recommendations in case of unconventional emergencies. It also proposes a solution for one possible and effective implementation of such a system. This chapter is a must-read before proceeding to any of chapters 4 through 7. Those chapters can then be read in parallel after the reader has completed chapter 3 and gone through the abstracts of those four chapters.

- The fourth chapter involves the development of the knowledge stores of the two domains under consideration, i.e., the Earthquake Knowledge Store (EKS) and the Terrorism Knowledge Store (TKS).

- Chapter 5 aims to develop an intelligent resource manager comprising a knowledge store along with procedures as a model for situation awareness, providing better interoperability of heterogeneous resources for emergency situation information. This resource manager supports end users in making the best decisions during an emergency by providing enhanced and real-time situation awareness to the general public.

- The sixth chapter focuses upon utilizing best practices—i.e., decision trees, ontological representation, case-based reasoning (CBR), and rule-based reasoning (RBR)—and demonstrates an ontology-supported hybrid reasoning framework for generating advice.

- Chapter 7 investigates the various aspects of the development and usage of multilingual and multimodal ontology.

- Finally, chapter 8 describes in detail a number of directions for researchers. The chapter is rounded off with an overall conclusion: that semantic technologies are quite relevant for the future of decision support, but several new developments are needed to reach its full potential.

Feedback, questions, and suggestions for improvement are always welcome. Please send them via email to jasarika@gmail.com.

                                                                            Sarika Jain

About the Author

Dr. Sarika Jain graduated from Jawaharlal Nehru University (India) in 2001. Her doctorate, awarded in 2011, is in the field of knowledge representation in Artificial Intelligence. She has served in the field of education for over 19 years and is currently in service at the National Institute of Technology, Kurukshetra (Institute of National Importance), India. Dr. Jain has authored or co-authored over 100 publications including books. Her current research interests are knowledge management and analytics, the semantic web, ontological engineering, and intelligent systems. She is currently working toward solving the interoperability problem generated by initiative in the internet of things, big data, and cloud computing.

Dr. Jain has supervised two doctoral scholars (five ongoing) who are now pursuing their postdoctoral studies, one in Spain and the other in Germany. Currently, she is guiding 15 students for their master's and doctoral research work in the area of knowledge representation. She serves as a reviewer for journals published by IEEE, Elsevier, and Springer. She has been involved as a program- and steering-committee member at many prestigious conferences in India and abroad.

She has two funded research projects: one ongoing, funded by CRIS-TEQIP-III and worth Rs 2.58 lakhs, and the other completed, funded by the Defense Research and Development Organization, India, and worth Rs 40 lakhs. She applied for a patent in November 2019. Dr. Jain has held various administrative positions at the department and institute level in her career, like head of department, hostel warden, faculty in charge of technical and cultural fests, member of research degree committee, and Center Incharge Examinations.

Dr. Jain has visited the United Kingdom and Singapore to present her research work. She has continuously supervised DAAD interns from different universities of Germany and many interns from India every summer. She works in collaboration with various researchers across the globe, including in Germany, Austria, Australia, Malaysia, the USA, and Romania. She has organized various challenges, conferences, and workshops, including the National Information Technology Conference (NITC), the Global Initiative of Academic Networks (GIAN) by the Ministry of Human Resource Development, Government of India, the International Conference on Smart Computing and Communication (ICSCC), the International Conference on Advanced Communication and Computational Technology (ICACCT), and International Conference on Eco-Friendly Computing and Communication Systems. She is a member of the Institute of Electrical and Electronics Engineers

(IEEE) and the Association for Computing Machinery (ACM) and a Life Member of the Computer Society of India (CSI), the International Association of Engineers (IAENG), and the International Association of Computer Science and Information Technology (IACSIT).

Dr. Jain is highly interested in worldwide collaborations and is seeking scholars and interns for her research group.

For the most up-to-date information, see https://sites.google.com/view/nitkkrsarikajain/.

Acknowledgment

I would like to express my deepest appreciation to those who provided me the possibility to initiate and then complete this book. My gratitude goes to my beloved and the strongest motivating factor of my success, my husband: Dr. Anuj Jain. I would like to acknowledge with much appreciation the crucial role of Ms. Sanju Tiwari, Ms. Sonia Mehla, Ms. Archana Patel, and my MCA graduate students who were instrumental during simulations of the prototypical system. The major part of the book was written while the project report of a funded research project was being written. All the ideas generated during discussion have sown the seeds of this book.

I thank the staff of Taylor and Francis for their support in bringing this book into existence. Thanks are due to the two anonymous reviewers for their constructive suggestions.

I thank my colleagues and PhD scholars at NIT Kurukshetra for proofreading the text. At the heart of these stands Prof. Ashutosh Kumar Singh, who provided me with a peaceful working environment.

Most importantly, I wish to thank my wonderful children, Bhavya and Sanyam, who always provide unending inspiration. I close my words by thanking the unmentioned individuals who are indirectly responsible and share the accomplishments.

Acronyms and Abbreviations

ADLs	Activities of Daily Living
AI	Artificial Intelligence
ATS	American Terrorism Study
JC3IEDM	Joint Consultation, Command and Control Information Exchange Data Model
C4ISR	Command, Control, Communications, Computers, Intelligence, Surveillance, and Reconnaissance
CEPEC	California Earthquake Prediction Evaluation Council
CONON	CONtextONtology
DARPA	Defense Advanced Research Projects Agency
DO4MG	Domain Ontology for Mass Gatherings
DSO	DSO National Laboratories
DSS	Decision Support System
ECDB	Extremist Crime Database
EDER	Earthquake Disaster Emergency Response
EKS	Earthquake Knowledge Store
EO	Earthquake Ontology
ETM-model	Economics of Terrorism Monitoring Model
GTD	Global Terrorism Database
IT	Information Technology
JMA	Japan Meteorological Agency
KDSAAS	Knowledge-Driven Situation Awareness and Advisory Support
KM	Knowledge Management
MDO	Meteorological Disaster Ontology
NAPO	Network Attack Planning Ontology
NMHS	National Meteorological and Hydrological Services
OLAP	Online Analytical Processing
OWA	Open-World Assumption
OWL	Web Ontology Language
PPT-US	Profiles of Perpetrators of Terrorism in the United States
RDF	Resource Description Framework
SAW	Situation Awareness
ST	Semantic Technology
SWRL	Semantic Web Rule Language
TKS	Terrorism Knowledge Store

TO	Terrorism Ontology
TTS	Terror Tracker System
WITS	Worldwide Incidents Tracking System
WWW	World Wide Web
XML	Extensible Markup Language

1

Semantics-based Decision Support - An Introduction

This book is an attempt to exploit the full potential of existing tools, techniques, and methodologies to provide situation awareness and advisory support to end-users in a seamless manner. The nature of information input to a Decision Support System (DSS) is majorly unstructured or semi-structured, making the decision-making process complex. The heterogeneity of information sources is easily dealt with by incorporating semantic technologies and hence facilitating intelligent situation awareness and decision support. This book presents to the reader the prototypical development of a knowledge-driven situation awareness and advisory support (KDSAAS) in the emergency domain. KDSAAS applies semantic technologies to provide real-time information in order to provide intelligent decision support. This introductory chapter advocates the importance and utilization of semantic data models in achieving semantic intelligence, which is a prerequisite for successful decision support systems. A few use cases demonstrating the importance of semantic technologies for decision support systems are also presented.

1.1 Decision Support

Decision making refers to the thought process of making a judgment to make a plan, solve a problem, react to a situation, or attain a goal. Decision making often involves argumentation, i.e., a process which involves thinking over alternative courses of action based on structured arguments. It involves becoming aware of and assessing the situations that may exist and events/actions that may take place. A decision support system (DSS) is required to assist the human counterparts in decision making by automating some of their tasks, i.e., by providing awareness of the situations and automated decision support. A DSS, also termed an advisory system, provides otherwise costly expertise and experience to human decision-makers in solving problems (which and how much resources to allocate, what actions to take, and others) [Inan et al. 2018, Jain 2018].

A DSS assists decision-makers at each level to achieve a scientific decision and improves the overall decision-making process. DSS research is very diverse and is influenced by various other areas, such as the social sciences. A DSS is composed of (i) the database (or knowledge base) that contains the relevant data; (ii) the model base and analytical tools to convert the data from the database to information; and (iii) the interface between the user and different components of the DSS.

Different authors have proposed different classifications of DSSs, none of which is accepted as a universal taxonomy. Based on the internal structure, a DSS can be classified as data-based, model-based, knowledge-based, communication-driven, or document-driven. A data-based DSS focuses on accessing and manipulating a large database for analysis purposes. A model-based DSS focuses on the application of models to solve a certain domain of problems, such as optimization, financial, or mathematical (simulation) models. In these DSSs, the model lies at the center and the data usage is minimal; the situation is analyzed by accessing and manipulating the model. A knowledge-based DSS is developed with the major focus on knowledge storage, representation, and management; it can suggest or recommend actions to managers. A communications-driven DSS concentrates on how people interact in groups and how decision making is done when a group of people collaborate and interact. A document-driven DSS analyzes a document collection, whether text or multimedia, to reach to a decision.

Most of these categories may be considered not as decision-oriented but rather as DSS tools. Based on the purpose of the DSS, they have been classified differently by different people, e.g., personal DSS (a DSS which focuses on and supports individuals), group DSS (a DSS which facilitates a group of people in reaching to a joint decision), negotiation DSS (a DSS in which negotiating is allowed on certain intermediate decisions), and business intelligence (a DSS performing data analysis of business information to convert it into actionable knowledge) [Arnott and Pervan 2005]. With the inclusion of Artificial Intelligence (AI) methods and techniques recently (fuzzy logic, knowledge bases, natural language programming (NLP), neural networks, genetic algorithms, and so forth), a lot of improvements can be seen in the working of DSSs. The new terminology thus common for DSSs is "Intelligent decision support systems." An Intelligent DSS is able to mimic human intelligence, performcommon-sense reasoning, and context-sensitive reasoning, hence improving the ability of decision-makers.

Knowledge-driven Intelligent DSS is the amalgamation of Knowledge Management (KM) and AI technologies to decision support. A knowledge-driven Intelligent DSS stores knowledge and assists humans in solving problems as any human companion would do. It has basically two components: a knowledge store with a representation scheme and an inference engine for reasoning.

1.2 Situation Awareness

Decision making is a stressful task, and it becomes even more stressful when thousands of lives depend on it. One of the important decision-makers in every nation is the government. At times, the government doesn't have an efficient way of finding resources such as trained professionals, medical services, rescue teams, and so on, when emergencies happen. When the decisions made are not the ones, many times it results in casualties which could have been avoided. Decision makers need to handle a very large and complex historical data store and quickly reach decisions. However, the way information is presented to them, and even the amount of information generated, may be so vague and inapposite that the decision-makers are not aware of the situation at hand. This leads to poor resource estimation and inaccurate action prediction, putting victims' lives at risk. For handling problems like these, a government needs an effective and efficient way to remove all the knowledge barriers from its path so that it can make quicker and more informed decisions to take advantage of the most opportunities to save lives and belongings [Kantorovitch et al. 2017, Nwiabu 2020].

Situation awareness is about being able to identify and process information. In a daily routine, situation awareness refers to the real-time minute-to-minute consciousness or perception of the whereabouts and minute details of the state of affairs in a given enterprise. A knowledge-driven Intelligent DSS has all the capabilities to represent and store knowledge in a manner that is required by decision-makers for making better decisions. The knowledge stores thus developed facilitate integrated information retrieval, which supports interoperability between different use cases for ease of management. They can store all historical events that have happened for a domain. These knowledge stores must be designed in a manner to overcome the problem of static and incomplete representation of knowledge, hence allowing better information sharing in an efficient and effective manner. Algorithms can then be developed for required use cases, such as providing situation awareness and resource management through browsing the knowledge, searching some concept in the knowledge stores, and submitting queries. This book provides a perspective on how semantic technologies (STs) can be used to narrate and outline situations, improving understanding and realization of the situation. STs give a detailed account of and portray the semantics that are related to information [Patel and Jain 2019].

1.3 Paradigm Shift from Data to Knowledge

In order to guide our actions and achieve desired goals, human beings need to connect pieces of information together. Similarly, machines need to climb the steps up the wisdom hierarchy (commonly called the DIKW pyramid). The DIKW pyramid shows the hierarchy from data to wisdom: data (raw facts), information (defining relationships), knowledge (explicit information), and wisdom (thinking and acting using knowledge) [Koltay 2020]. Some applications require a combination of different domain knowledge to solve problems so that an appropriate action or conclusion can be deduced. However, combining domain knowledge is a very complex task, and it requires too much memory and time if the information is not organized in a proper format. A large amount of data comes from different places, which generates heterogeneity problem. The heterogeneity of data produces variation in meaning or ambiguity in the interpretation of entities; as a result, it prevents information sharing between systems. Therefore, without identification of the semantic mappings between entities, we cannot communicate, interact, collaborate, or share information across applications or use different knowledge sources in one application. Various approaches have been proposed to achieve solutions to these problems, but achieving optimal performance remains an open challenge. We need to convert data into knowledge artifacts to achieve interoperability; the most critical success factor is efficient and effective knowledge sharing across applications, organizations, and decision-makers, which in turn requires KM techniques.

Knowledge Management refers to collecting, processing, and organizing knowledge. The way information is organized has an effect on the processes or operations that are used to manipulate the entities of the information [Evangelou et al. 2005]. McCarthy[1] in 1955 coined the term "Artificial Intelligence" for the capacity that allows machines to behave as intelligently as human beings. All the components of a DSS—the knowledge base, the model base, and the user interface—employ KM and AI techniques. These techniques help by improving the critical thinking of experts and recommending the next course of action [Bughin et al. 2017, Gasser and Almeida 2017]. This develops competitive intelligence, retaining employees' expertise and sharing best practices. Formalization of knowledge is a question of both structure and function. Real-world problems use real-time systems that are resource constrained: they should work very effectively and accurately within the given resource for the system response. For any intelligent machine, the focus is on the representation of knowledge in such a manner that inferences can be drawn efficiently and effectively within the resource constraints (data, time, space, etc.). For decades, in order to

---

[1]   https://en.wikipedia.org/wiki/Artificial_intelligence.

interface with real-world objects and enable cooperation between applications and services, it has been the duty of human counterparts to understand semantics (meaning) and make it machine processable. To plan and integrate existing data resources and make them shareable, we need to model semantics.

Though traditional data models scale well for many core data integration and storage requirements, they are often unable to cope with the dynamic nature of today's world. This is where STs excel, as they build upon the semantic data model (the Resource Description Framework, RDF). Semantic technologies aim at augmenting the web technologies of today by finding and taking slices of data sets from different places, aggregating them, and analyzing them in a more straightforward, powerful way. Ontology (the heart of STs) provides an organizing mechanism such that knowledge is managed to be accessible to software agents as well as humans. STs aid in building artificially intelligent knowledge-based systems, as they help machines integrate and process resources contextually and intelligently [Tahamtan 2017, Hendler 2001][2]. Semantic data models create interoperable data stores and facilitate the development of intelligent applications to provide resource-management assistance and situation awareness in order to enable real-time recommendations and decision support.

1.4 Intelligence and Semantics

The work that humans need to do is growing day by day; therefore, the assistance of machines is not enough. Machines should be made capable of learning and thinking in order to enhance and support human activities in an intelligent manner.

1.4.1 Understanding Semantics

Human beings understand each other's communication by understanding words and phrases and the relationships between them in the presence of accumulated knowledge. This accumulated knowledge enables humans to react in different contexts. In addition to how understanding situations is changed by different contexts, the same sentence can have different meanings in different contexts. Understanding a communication involves more than words—words are just the symbols. Words put together with accumulated knowledge and context will provide the required comprehension as well as the correct interpretation. That's semantics: understanding both the meaning

---

[2] https://en.wikipedia.org/wiki/Artificial_intelligence.

and elucidation, i.e., the interpretation of symbols, words, signs, and sentence structure put together. Semantics clarifies the sense of a sentence by constructing a relation between the adjoining words.

Semantics provides unambiguous meaning to the content, making it search-engine friendly and internationally accessible. It also provides interoperability to content, allowing the exchange and use of information across different platforms and devices. The information-technology (IT) world of today comprises many operating systems, many high-level languages, many different types of networks, and so on. From both data and application perspectives, more machine-interpretable and explicit semantics is necessary in the loosely coupled world of today.

1.4.2 Semantic Intelligence

The human brain is a very complex framework that enables a person to think and behave intelligently. It instructs the whole body by sending information via neurons and accumulates the information that functions as background knowledge. Humans decide upon a course of action based on past experience, gathered knowledge, and the current scenario. By contrast, machines try every possible combination but are limited to figuring out a perfect answer in the current context to the problem at hand. It befits us, in designing automated systems, to represent and make inferences with such imperfect knowledge. Intelligent systems are the computer-based approach to decision making. Intelligence is required to integrate workflows and provide the insight necessary to stay informed and act decisively. There is a semantic gap in the way humans anticipate things and perform some task and the way their machine counterparts do. Imagine a machine looking at an image as we humans do!

AI pioneer Herbert A. Simon (1965)[3] of Carnegie Mellon University predicted that within the next 20 years, machines would become capable of doing any sort of work a human can do. Machines today are not able to comprehend our speech and texts. What intelligent machines suffer from the most today is a lack of the common-sense knowledge which we humans use in our everyday speech and writing. Apart from this, AI is rich enough in the ability to solve isolated problems based on isolated data silos. The question is, can a machine think and behave intelligently just like a human? Of course, if it has an intelligent data model that provides the enriched meaning of the real-world entities. To achieve this vision, various data models have been proposed. The choice of data model affects the reasoning process, which determines the semantic relationship between the entities. A machine will behave intelligently if the underlying representation scheme exhibits knowledge that can be achieved by

---

[3] https://en.wikipedia.org/wiki/History_of_artificial_intelligence.

representing semantics. Semantic intelligence focuses on information rather than process. Sharing the understanding and semantics of information concepts provides semantic intelligence to a business or process automatically. Semantic intelligence helps us make sense of the most vital resource—i.e., data—by making it interpretable and meaningful. For whatever application the data will be put to, it must be represented in a manner that is understandable to the machine and hence usable by the human. All the important relationships (including who, what, when, where, how, and why) in the required data from any heterogeneous data sources must be made explicit. Developing better insight into data enables better understanding, thus supporting better information sharing and reuse for better decision making. Semantic intelligence refers to filling the semantic gap between the understanding of humans and of machines by making a machine look at everything in terms of object-oriented concepts, as humans look at it—meaning that a machine should look at an image not as a collection of pixels but as a collection of objects. Semantic intelligence possesses the following significant characteristics:

1. *Semantically Rich Data:* The quality of data is the first focus of semantic intelligence. As opposed to only simple relationships, as in the case of a relational-database management system, semantic intelligence exploits more complex relationships by virtue of semantic data models.

2. *Semantic Data Model:* The ontologies serve as the data model bridging the gap between structured and unstructured data.

3. *Data as a Service:* Semantic intelligence must provide a platform for enterprise-wide knowledge collaboration. Linked data serves this purpose and can be used as training data for machine learning algorithms.

4. *No Mystery:* Explainable AI has been known as a concept for years. Semantic intelligence focuses on explaining concepts.

5. *Toward self-optimizing machines:* In a virtuous cycle, machine learning feeds the ontologies and, in return, ontologies can help to improve machine learning algorithms by providing better feature extraction and better precision. Once fed, systems with semantic intelligence work like self-optimizing machines.

Consider an example of some information available readily on the web and understandable by humans but not machines, like the calendar, statistics, weather forecasts, product catalogues, or train schedules. It is not at all possible to pull out required pieces of data from this information in a reproducible and reusable format. As another example, a keyword or phrasal search is intrinsically unintelligent; it just matches the keywords in documents and lists the outcomes. Where is the intelligence? It comes automatically with semantically rich data. In this way, semantic intelligence matches the understanding of humans and machines.

1.5 Intersection of STs and DSS

STs have extended the capabilities of DSSs to a very large number of users. This book envisions semantics-based DSS as applying AI, KM, and STs to DSS. The triangulation of AI, KM, and STs has gone a long way in overcoming the challenges faced by DSS.

Both DSS and STs can be seen as descendants of AI [Futia and Vetrò 2020]. STs are emerging as a core enabler and a significant DSS development platform [Moreno 2009, Antunes et al. 2014]. They are now not in their infancy, as they are maturing and standards have emerged that allow them to be deployed broadly across the IT industry for all fields of interest and for all domains. Every facet of industry or business can be transformed by utilizing semantically rich information, as it fuels the knowledge network where computers can store, access, understand, and reuse information automatically. Semantic data models offer the potential of executing a wide range of tasks quickly and leading to accurate decisions.

Semantics-based DSS lies at the intersection of STs and knowledge-driven Intelligent DSS. Vocabularies, thesauruses, or ontologies provide definitions of the concepts (also referred to as terms) that are used in a specific application, define and characterize the relations among concepts, and define any possible restrictions in utilizing those concepts. Ontology as an ST is an effective tool for capturing knowledge and the backbone of semantics-based DSS [Thuan et al. 2018, Khantong and Ahmad 2019]. Ontologies provide strategic advantages on the basis of the multifaceted needs of DSSs:

- Preserve the semantics across databases and applications with possibly distinct requirements but common shared semantics.
- Support seamless semantic interoperability at operational, tactical, and strategic levels of an enterprise or government system.
- Handle the heterogeneity of data by allowing encoding of all involved knowledge in a uniform format, facilitating the modularity and extensibility of the system.
- Provide a common platform for integrating disparate and diverse information sources required for a common task.
- Ease content management and classification by defining a standardized and common vocabulary, thus providing structure to the

knowledge of a specific domain characterized by the concept hierarchies.

- Capture the most complex thoughts about the concepts in the form of relations, properties, constraints, and rules.
- Facilitate effective query answering and reasoning with explanation from structured through semi-structured to unstructured problems.
- Make the semantics explicit and represent human knowledge in a machine-understandable manner.
- Ease the introduction of new requirements and functions to any system without major rewriting of code.

Within this environment that STs provide, intelligent agents are able to solve unstructured and complicated problems because they are able to represent and store information from disparate means on a common platform and reason around in accordance with the requirements of decision-makers. Thus, STs are deemed suitable for well-informed decision support. A semantics-based DSS has three components all fed by STs and integrated in such a way as to accomplish a concrete (business) purpose:

1. The Knowledge Base: The data and knowledge component—i.e., the ontology-based schema and instance base developed for representing and storing domain knowledge required by the DSS.
2. The Model Base: The algorithmic component, which is augmented with rules that generate recommendations and provide the required decision support.
3. The User Interface: The user-to-system interaction component, involving the exchange of information between the user and system and providing the result of the DSS computation as the output.

In this manner, STs cover all the phases of a DSS from collecting, representing, and storing the information through formulating and processing the decision-making problem to presenting the decisions to the stakeholders.

1.6 Sample Use Cases

Applications of STs for decision making are scattered around various interesting domains, e.g., healthcare systems and medicine, ecology, law, road safety, public services including personnel safety, wastewater management, customer service, emergency management, and many more [Rockwell et al.

2009, Borsje et al. 2008, Kokar et al. 2009, Berlanga et al. 2012, Sheng et al. 2020, Dissanayake et al. 2020, Stearns et al. 2001, Mishra and Jain 2019, Patel et al. 2018, Patel et al. 2019, Mishra and Jain 2020]. STs support information-system processes e-government, business intelligence, social networking and collaboration support, clinical management, information retrieval and KM, information integration and sharing, situation awareness, web-service annotation and discovery, data-warehouse performance improvement, and simulation systems. A few use cases and case studies follow here [Baker et al. 2001].

1.6.1 E-Government

Through the use of STs, the Center for Biosecurity and Public Health Informatics Research at the University of Texas Health Science Center at Houston designed and built a public health surveillance system in order to recognize and acknowledge the health-related problems of the community. As an another instance, Ordnance Survey—the national mapping agency of the United Kingdom—maintains and enhances its database (the largest geospatial database in the world) using STs to enable customers to query, understand, and integrate the data more easily, accurately, and cost-effectively [Shan et al. 2012].

1.6.2 Healthcare

STs have been largely utilized to support decision-making functions in all aspects of healthcare, from prediction of disease to follow-up. They help standardize medical activities, as a result of which the quality of healthcare is drastically improved. STs have been utilized in the assessment of risk to reduce medical errors, thus reducing healthcare service costs. Using STs, PharmaSURVEYOR is able to compose safer drug regimens, benefiting society at large.

Researchers at Agfa HealthCare Belgium worked toward reducing errors in radiological procedure orders. They banked upon integrating the cross-domain knowledge and explanations provided by the proof engines, which helped clinicians in decision support. The approach helped reduce the error rate, as clinicians were then not overlooking vital facts because of voluminous data [Mishra et al. 2018, Dalal et al. 2019].

1.6.3 Understanding Natural Language

STs facilitate natural-language interfaces with business applications. A conversational system called NATAS has been developed at Tata Consultancy Services, India, which users can interact with in their natural language [Maynard et al. 2016].

1.6.4 IT Service

Semantics-based DSSs support information services across companies as well as covering the whole life cycle of IT projects. Strategic IT management is governed by semantic tools.

1.6.5 Tourism

The introduction of STs in the tourism industry makes possible the interoperation and management of semantically diverse data from disparate sources. CRUZAR is a semantic web application developed for the city of Zaragoza in Spain. It prepares itineraries for visitors according to their profiles and desires, as well as having some predefined itineraries.

1.6.6 Oil and Gas Industry

Rich ontologies and knowledge bases exist in the oil and gas industry. The current standards in STs can be leveraged to map those ontologies and provide a unified framework. This will result in a meaningful metadata reflecting the domain concepts. The utilization of STs will facilitate easy integration, extension, and reuse.

1.6.7 Education

The use of ontology in the education sector can help achieve "anytime, anywhere, anybody learning," as it provides information which is understandable and processable by computers. Video collections of dancers, for example, can be annotated in order to locate certain segments of choreography. STs have the potential to extend and transform teaching and learning, particularly in those educational settings in which learners are encouraged to engage with 'authentic' data from multiple sources (Cranmer 2016). The Ensemble project, part of the joint ESRC/EPSRCfunded Technology Enhanced Learning (TEL) programme, explored the role of 'semantic web' technologies to support undergraduate and postgraduate teaching in complex and rapidly-evolving fields where case-based learning is common. As part of the Ensemble project, the researchers used the power of STs in education on contemporary dance (Martinez-Garcia et al. 2011).

Resource lists or course reserves of reading material are companions for students. Talis Information Limited, in collaboration with the University of Plymouth (UK), developed an ST-enabled resource list management tool providing use cases for both instructors and students.

1.6.8 Medicine

The China Academy of Chinese Medicine Sciences used STs to share and reuse data across databases and organizational boundaries. This helped in unifying and linking relational data. The academy has also developed a search and query system for navigating around an extensible set of databases.

1.6.9 Customer Service

Customer service directly affects the potential profitability of an enterprise. STs cover all facets of customer service, from inquiry to after sales. At early stages, semantics-based DSSs can help enterprises better respond to customer inquiries, delivery dates, and selling prices, finally converting these inquiries into customer orders. DSSs utilizing STs have also come into the picture to improve after-sales service.

1.6.10 NASA

STs have been applied to NASA mission needs and are dispersed across different NASA centers. Semantics-based DSS supports distributed NASA teams of scientists, engineers, accident investigators, etc., by providing them with situation awareness through a customizable, semantically structured information repository based on shared ontologies.

1.6.11 Law

STs can help newly recruited judges answer complex legal questions and facilitate exploration of the database of concluded cases and their judgements. Such a case-law system has been developed by the Autonomous University of Barcelona for the Spanish General Council of the Judiciary.

The Korea Institute of Science and Technology Information, in collaboration with the Korean Ministry of Justice, has come up with an intelligent and systematic legislation support system for analyzing legislative information.

1.6.12 News

The Hermes news portal is a semantic-based DSS that extracts and presents relevant news items from various sources for decision support. SemNews, in collaboration with OntoSem, extracts news items from the Internet and stores them structurally. MyPlanet is also an ontology-based, personalized news classification system.

1.6.13 Big Fish in the Market

As is obvious by now, STs are the heart of DSS. Through applying STs, a multitude of benefits crop up facilitating decision support. Even the major players in today's market are utilizing STs for their businesses, including IBM (the Watson system) [Ferrucci et al. 2010], the *New York Times*, Thomson Reuters, Google (KnowItAll and many others), Yahoo (SearchMonkey), the BBC [Raimond et al. 2010], Citigroup, Oracle (Seamark Navigator), Hewlett-Packard, Radar Networks, and Cycorp.

1.7 Case Study

In this section, a semantics-based DSS for unconventional emergencies is conceived using cutting-edge IT tools and semantic techniques to lower, if not resolve, the impacts of catastrophic disasters. The whole environment has been simulated for two types of emergencies, one natural (earthquake) and the other created (terrorism).

1.7.1 Unconventional Emergencies

A disaster is either a natural (like an earthquake) or a created (like terrorism) emergency that affects the livelihood, life, and property of individuals and groups of people. A disaster may cause casualty at a mass scale, and recovery may take years. Applying STs to disaster management can enable better situation awareness and decision support by providing data interoperability among systems, providing relevant information, facilitating communication among the stakeholders, and generating better resource estimation and recommendations [Mehla and Jain 2019, Patel et al. 2020]. An ST-enabled resource manager and recommendation system will significantly improve the management of disasters and effectively minimize casualties.

1.7.2 The State of the Art

Various recent studies and systems have focused on applying STs in the domain of disaster management for providing situation awareness and decision support. Some noteworthy works from the last five years are listed in Table 1.1.

Disaster-strike information is scattered in various forms, like web articles, databases, knowledge bases, video, and audio. Web articles such as on Wikipedia, news sites, etc., contain almost all of the information, but they are static documents that require reading through multiple pages to understand a single incident, and decision making requires analyzing more than a single

TABLE 1.1

The State of the Art

Reference	Title
Moreira (2019)	"SEMIoTICS: Semantic Model-Driven Development for IoT Interoperability of Emergency Services: Improving the Semantic Interoperability of IoT Early Warning Systems"
Bannour et al. (2019)	"Ontology-Based Representation of Crisis Response Situations"
Maalel and Ghézala (2019)	"Towards a Collaborative Approach to Decision Making Based on Ontology and Multi-Agent System Application to Crisis Management"
Mehla and Jain (2020)	"An Ontology Supported Hybrid Approach for Recommendation in Emergency Situations"
Mehla and Jain (2019)	"Development and Evaluation of Knowledge Treasure for Emergency Situation Awareness"
Ahmad et al. (2019)	"A Semantic Ontology for Disaster Trail Management System"
Kontopoulos et al. (2018)	"Ontology-Based Representation of Crisis Management Procedures for Climate Events"
Bouyerbou et al. (2019)	"Geographic Ontology for Major Disasters: Methodology and Implementation"
Inan et al. (2018)	"Developing a Decision Support System for Disaster Management: Case Study of an Indonesia Volcano Eruption"
Moreira et al. (2017)	"Ontology-Driven Conceptual Modeling for Early Warning Systems: Redesigning the Situation Modeling Language"
Simas et al. (2017)	"A Data Exchange Tool Based on Ontology for Emergency Response Systems"
Anbarasi and Mayilvahanan (2017)	"Humanitarian Assistance Ontology Implementation during Disaster Management in Chennai Flood-2015 Using Text Mining Techniques"
Poblet et al. (2018)	"Crowdsourcing Roles, Methods and Tools for Data-Intensive Disaster Management"
Wang et al. (2017)	"E-patroller: A Semantic Technology-Based Public Emergency Monitoring System"
Pandey and Bansal (2017)	"A Semantic Safety Check System for Emergency Management"
Zhong et al. (2016)	"Emergency Decision of Meteorological Disasters: A Geo-Ontology Based Perspective"
Hassan and Chen-Burger (2016)	"A Communication and Tracking Ontology for Mobile Systems in the Event of a Large Scale Disaster"
Apisakmontri et al. (2016)	"An Ontology-Based Framework for Semantic Reconciliation in Humanitarian Aid in Emergency Information Systems"
Poslad et al. (2015)	"A Semantic IoT Early Warning System for Natural Environment Crisis Management"

event to draw patterns. Video can explain an event very clearly and properly, but the problem is that not every incident makes it to the web in video format—for the creation of video, a creator needs full details of the event and a lot of time for editing, which is not feasible given the number of incidents.

1.7.3 Managerial Implications (Benefits)

A community can be exposed to a wide variety of disasters, both natural and created, such as earthquakes, fires, and acts of terrorism. Preparing for the next disaster can help humanity survive and recover. Earthquakes are inevitable, but damage is not, and terrorism can never be defeated by military means alone. State and local governments have the primary responsibility for planning and managing the consequences of a disaster using available resources in critical hours. A knowledge-driven situation awareness and advisory support (KDSAAS) is an effort at creating the largest comprehensive knowledge base of earthquake and terrorism and related activities, the people and agencies involved, and extremist movements, and providing a platform to society, the government, and military personnel in order to combat the evolving global menace. This knowledge store is continuously updated with all available information. This section highlights managerial implications and how KSDAAS helps society, military personnel, and the government in tackling these threats.

1.7.3.1 Government

The government needs to adopt a comprehensive and inclusive approach. Timely access to critical information has always been essential and the strongest necessity for any task of government. This tool will provide decision support to the government at the strategic level.

- Before a Disaster: This tool will enable the development of more efficient and effective policies, budgets, rules, and regulations. These will greatly help any nation through rough times. Good policy is that which does not create a bottleneck, those rules or administration practices that create a barrier in smooth operation.
- During a Disaster: Officials can use this tool to perform various operations and for decision support. Resource allocation can be done based on resource availability which can be fetched from the knowledge base.

1.7.3.2 Military Personnel

With more prepared forces we can also ensure the safety of our protectors who risk their lives to save ours. This tool will provide decision support to the military personnel who directly tackle the situation.

- Before a Disaster: The officials are able to know the available resources in real time, hence able to control the pace of resource acquisition. This will make them better ready for future disasters.
- During a Disaster: Military personnel will feel confident when they are better equipped with the know-how and history from every disaster.

1.7.3.3 Society

A more informed public means that we have millions of eyes working together to keep everybody safe, and the public knows everything and has ways to react, handle situations, and keep themselves safe until properly trained forces are on the scene to assist. This is a valuable addition to national security. All parts of society, including women and young people, need to come forward and be educated to be able to save themselves in adverse situations. Through making judicious use of this tool, the public can be trained and become better aware of situations.

- Before a Disaster: All the material and information available will be realistic, reliable, and usable. Society can be given teaching and training about various terrorist groups, non-governmental organizations, and how to react if they become victims themselves. The society becomes aware of all the incidents that have happened in the country.
- During a Disaster: Users can access all essential information required during a disaster, like emergency help-line numbers and the nearest army and police camps. All information will be updated according to real data.

With time, these problems of earthquakes and terrorism will diminish or have little or no effect on our society, be it the lives of people, the economy, or the infrastructure.

KDSAAS will achieve these responsibilities of the government and raise awareness of the potential challenges. The innovation of this tool in comparison with existing ontology tools has several aspects, because it is specifically designed with the needs of non-computer experts in mind. KDSAAS is intended to satisfy the following criteria:

- It is accessible to the users whether they are familiar with formal logic notation or not.
- All the operations and interactions are as simple as possible and require no more than a simple introduction.
- The presentation (hierarchical and textual) of the concepts is natural.
- The logical representations or inferences coming from the emergency knowledge base are transparent to the user.

References

Ahmad, Ashfaq, Roslina Othman, Mohamad Fauzan, and Qazi Mudassar Ilyas. "A semantic ontology for disaster trail management system." *International Journal of Advanced Computer Science and Applications* 10, no. 10 (2019): 77–90.

Anbarasi, C., and P. Mayilvahanan. "Humanitarian assistance ontology implementation during disaster management in Chennai flood-2015 using text mining techniques." *International Journal of Pure and Applied Mathematics* 116, no. 21 (2017): 729–739.

Antunes, Francisco, Manuela Freire, and João Paulo Costa. "Semantic web tools and decision-making." In *Group Decision and Negotiation: A Process Oriented View—Joint INFORMS-GDN and EWG-DSS International Conference, GDN 2014*, pp. 270–277. Springer, Cham, Switzerland, 2014.

Apisakmontri, Pasinee, Ekawit Nantajeewarawat, Mitsuru Ikeda, and Marut Buranarach. "An ontology-based framework for semantic reconciliation in humanitarian aid in emergency information systems." *Journal of Information Processing* 24, no. 1 (2016): 73–82.

Arnott, David, and Graham Pervan. "A critical analysis of decision support systems research." *Journal of Information Technology* 20, no. 2 (2005): 67–87.

Baker, Thomas, Natasha Noy, Ralph Swick, and Ivan Herman. Semantic Web Case Studies and Use Cases. World Wide Web Consortium. Available at https://www.w3.org/2001/sw/sweo/public/UseCases/ (last accessed on 15.03.2020).

Bannour, Walid, Ahmed Maalel, and Henda Hajjami Ben Ghezala. "Ontology-based representation of crisis response situations." In *Computational Collective Intelligence: ICCCI 2019*, pp. 417–427. Springer, Cham, Switzerland, 2019.

Berlanga, Rafael, Oscar Romero, Alkis Simitsis, Victoria Nebot, Torben Bach Pedersen, Alberto Abelló, and María José Aramburu. "Semantic web technologies for business intelligence." In *Business Intelligence Applications and the Web: Models, Systems and Technologies*, pp. 310–339. IGI Global, Hershey, PA, 2012.

Borsje, Jethro, Leonard Levering, and Flavius Frasincar. "Hermes: a semantic web-based news decision support system." In *Proceedings of the 2008 ACM Symposium on Applied Computing*, pp. 2415–2420. ACM, New York, NY, 2008.

Bouyerbou, Hafidha, Kamal Bechkoum, and Richard Lepage. "Geographic ontology for major disasters: methodology and implementation." *International Journal of Disaster Risk Reduction* 34 (2019): 232–242.

Bughin, Jacques, Eric Hazan, Sree Ramaswamy, Michael Chui, Tera Allas, Peter Dahlström, Nicolaus Henke, et al. *Artificial Intelligence: The Next Digital Frontier?* McKinsey Global Institute, Washington, DC, 2017.

Dalal, Sumit, Sarika Jain, and Mayank Dave. "A systematic review of smart mental healthcare." In *Proceedings of the 5th International Conference on Cyber Security & Privacy in Communication Networks (ICCS) 2019*. Available at SSRN 3511013 (2019).

Cranmer, S., N.B., Dohn, M., de Laat, T., Ryberg, and J.A., Sime (eds). "Semantic web learning technology design: addressing pedagogical challenges and precarious futures." *Proceedings of the 10th International Conference on Networked Learning 2016*, 2016. ISBN: ISBN 978-1-86220-324-2.

Dissanayake, Pavithra I., Tiago K. Colicchio, and James J. Cimino. "Using clinical reasoning ontologies to make smarter clinical decision support systems: a systematic review and data synthesis." *Journal of the American Medical Informatics Association* 27, no. 1 (2020): 159–174.

Evangelou, Christina, Nikos Karacapilidis, and Omar Abou Khaled. "Interweaving knowledge management, argumentation and decision making in a collaborative setting: the KAD ontology model." *International Journal of Knowledge and Learning* 1, no. 1–2 (2005): 130–145.

Ferrucci, David, Eric Brown, Jennifer Chu-Carroll, James Fan, David Gondek, Aditya A. Kalyanpur, Adam Lally, et al. "Building Watson: an overview of the DeepQA project." *AI Magazine* 31, no. 3 (2010): 59–79.

Futia, Giuseppe, and Antonio Vetrò. "On the integration of knowledge graphs into deep learning models for a more comprehensible AI—three challenges for future research." *Information* 11, no. 2 (2020): 122.

Gasser, Urs, and Virgilio A. F. Almeida. "A layered model for AI governance." *IEEE Internet Computing* 21, no. 6 (2017): 58–62.

Hassan, Mohd Khairul Azmi, and Yun-Heh Chen-Burger. "A communication and tracking ontology for mobile systems in the event of a large scale disaster." In *Agent and Multi-Agent Systems: Technology and Applications*, pp. 119–137. Springer, Cham, Switzerland, 2016.

Hendler, James. "Agents and the semantic web." *IEEE Intelligent Systems* 16, no. 2 (2001): 30–37.

Inan, Dedi I., Ghassan Beydoun, and Biswajeet Pradhan. "Developing a decision support system for disaster management: case study of an Indonesia volcano eruption." *International Journal of Disaster Risk Reduction* 31 (2018): 711–721.

Jain, Sarika. "Intelligent decision support for unconventional emergencies." In *Exploring Intelligent Decision Support Systems*, pp. 199–219. Springer, Cham, Switzerland, 2018.

Kantorovitch, Julia, Ilkka Niskanen, Jarmo Kalaoja, and Toni Staykova. "Designing situation awareness addressing the needs of medical emergency response." In *ICSOFT 2017—Proceedings of the 12th International Conference on Software Technologies*, pp. 467–472. SciTePress, Setúbal, Portugal, 2017.

Khantong, Sommai, and Mohammad Nazir Ahmad. "An ontology for sharing and managing information in disaster response: in flood response usage scenarios." *Journal on Data Semantics* 9 (2019): 39–52.

Kokar, Mieczyslaw M., Christopher J. Matheus, and Kenneth Baclawski. "Ontology-based situation awareness." *Information Fusion* 10, no. 1 (2009): 83–98.

Koltay, Tibor. "Quality of open research data: values, convergences and governance." *Information* 11, no. 4 (2020): 175.

Kontopoulos, Efstratios, Panagiotis Mitzias, Jürgen Moßgraber, Philipp Hertweck, Hylke van der Schaaf, Désirée Hilbring, Francesca Lombardo, et al. "Ontology-based representation of crisis management procedures for climate events." In *Proceedings of the 15th ISCRAM Conference*, pp. 1064–1073. Rochester Institute of Technology, Rochester, NY, 2018.

Maalel, Ahmed, and Henda Ben Ghézala. "Towards a collaborative approach to decision making based on ontology and multi-agent system application to crisis management." *Procedia Computer Science* 164 (2019): 193–198.

Martinez-Garcia Agustina, Simon Morris, Michael Tscholl, and Patrick Carmichael. "Case-based learning, pedagogical innovation, and semantic web technologies." *IEEE Transactions on Learning Technologies* 5, no. 2 (2011): 104–116.

Maynard, Diana, Kalina Bontcheva, and Isabelle Augenstein. "Natural language processing for the semantic web." *Synthesis Lectures on the Semantic Web: Theory and Technology* 6, no. 2 (2016): 1–194.

Mehla, Sonia, and Sarika Jain. "Development and evaluation of knowledge treasure for emergency situation awareness." *International Journal of Computers and Applications* (2019): 1–11.

Mehla, Sonia, and Sarika Jain. "An Ontology Supported Hybrid Approach for Recommendation in Emergency Situations." *Annals of Telecommunications* (2020) ISSN: 0003-4347 (Print) 1958–9395 (Online). In Print.

Mishra Tiwari, Sanju, Sarika Jain, Ajith Abraham, and Smita Shandilya. "Secure semantic smart healthcare (S3HC)." *Journal of Web Engineering* 17, no. 8 (2018): 617–646.

Mishra, Sanju, and Sarika Jain. "Ontologies as a semantic model in IoT." *International Journal of Computers and Applications* 42, no. 3 (2020): 233–243.

Mishra, Sanju, and Sarika Jain. "An intelligent knowledge treasure for military decision support." *International Journal of Web-Based Learning and Teaching Technologies* 14, no. 3 (2019): 55–75.

Moreira, João Luiz Rebelo, Luís Ferreira Pires, Marten van Sinderen, and Patricia Dockhorn Costa. "Ontology-driven conceptual modeling for early warning systems: redesigning the situation modeling language." In *Proceedings of the 5th International Conference on Model-Driven Engineering and Software Development (MODELSWARD 2017)*, pp. 467–477. SciTePress, Setúbal, Portugal, 2017.

Moreira, João Luiz Rebelo. *SEMIoTICS: Semantic Model-driven Development for IoT Interoperability of Emergency Services—Improving the Semantic Interoperability of IoT Early Warning Systems*. PhD diss., University of Twente, Enschede, the Netherlands, 2019.

Moreno, Juan Antonio Bernabé. *Semantic web meets competitive intelligence*. University of Granada, Granada, Spain, 2019.

Nwiabu, Nuka D. *Situation awareness approach to context-aware case-based decision support*. PhD diss., Robert Gordon University, Aberdeen, UK, 2020.

Pandey, Yogesh and Bansal Srividya Kona. A semantic safety check system for emergency management. *Open Journal of Semantic Web (OJSW)*, 4 (2017): 35–50.

Patel, Archana, and Sarika Jain. "Present and future of semantic web technologies: a research statement." *International Journal of Computers and Applications* (2019): 1–10. DOI: 10.1080/1206212X.2019.1570666.

Patel, Archana, Sarika Jain, and Shishir K. Shandilya. "Data of semantic web as unit of knowledge." *Journal of Web Engineering* 17, no. 8 (2018): 647–674.

Patel, Archana, Abhisek Sharma and Sarika Jain. "An intelligent resource manager over terrorism knowledge base." *Recent Patents on Computer Science* 12 (2019): 1–12.

Patel, Archana, Umesh Kumar Yadav, and Sarika Jain. "Non-monotonic reasoning for scenario awareness over emergency knowledge base." In *Proceedings of ICETIT 2019*, pp. 482–489. Springer, Cham, Switzerland, 2020.

Poblet, Marta, Esteban García-Cuesta, and Pompeu Casanovas. "Crowdsourcing roles, methods and tools for data-intensive disaster management." *Information Systems Frontiers* 20, no. 6 (2018): 1363–1379.

Poslad, Stefan, Stuart E. Middleton, Fernando Chaves, Ran Tao, Ocal Necmioglu, and Ulrich Bügel. "A semantic IoT early warning system for natural environment crisis management." *IEEE Transactions on Emerging Topics in Computing* 3, no. 2 (2015): 246–257.

Raimond, Yves, Tom Scott, Silver Oliver, Patrick Sinclair, and Michael Smethurst. "Use of semantic web technologies on the BBC web sites." In *Linking Enterprise Data*, pp. 263–283. Springer, Boston, MA, 2010.

Rockwell, Justin, Ian R. Grosse, Sundar Krishnamurty, and Jack C. Wileden. "A Decision Support Ontology for collaborative decision making in engineering design." In *2009 International Symposium on Collaborative Technologies and Systems*, pp. 1–9. IEEE, Los Alamitos, CA, 2009.

Rospocher, Marco, and Luciano Serafini. "Ontology-centric decision support." In *Proceedings of the International Workshop on Semantic Technologies Meet Recommender Systems & Big Data*, pp. 61–72. 2012.

Shan, Siqing, Li Wang, Ling Li, and Yong Chen. "An emergency response decision support system framework for application in e-government." *Information Technology and Management* 13, no. 4 (2012): 411–427.

Sheng, Yin, Xi Chen, Haijian Mo, Xin Chen, and Yang Zhang. "An ontology for decision-making support in air traffic management." In *Artificial Intelligence in China*, pp. 458–466. Springer, Singapore, 2020.

Simas, Félix, Rebeca Barros, Laís Salvador, Marian Weber, and Simone Amorim. "A data exchange tool based on ontology for emergency response systems." In *Metadata and Semantics Research: MTSR 2017*, pp. 74–79. Springer, Cham, Switzerland, 2017.

Stearns, Michael Q., Colin Price, Kent A. Spackman, and Amy Y. Wang. "SNOMED clinical terms: overview of the development process and project status." In *Proceedings of the AMIA Symposium*, pp. 662–666. American Medical Informatics Association, Bethesda, MD, 2001.

Simon, H. A. (1965). The Shape of Automation for Men and Management, New York: Harper & Row.

Tahamtan, Nick. *How semantic technologies enable domain experts to steer cognitive applications.* IDC White Paper CEMA42878117. IDC, Framingham, MA, 2017.

Thuan, Nguyen Hoang, Pedro Antunes, and David Johnstone. "A decision tool for business process crowdsourcing: ontology, design, and evaluation." *Grxoup Decision and Negotiation* 27, no. 2 (2018): 285–312.

Wang, Yaojun, Gao, Yang, and Yang, Beijing. E-patroller: A semantic technology-based public emergency monitoring system, *In 2017 IEEE 2nd International Conference on Big Data Analysis (ICBDA)*, pp. 250–253. IEEE. March 2017.

Zhong, Shao-bo, Chao-lin Wang, Guan-nan Yao, and Quan-yi Huang. "Emergency decision of meteorological disasters: a geo-ontology based perspective." In *2016 International Conference on Computational Modeling, Simulation and Applied Mathematics (CMSAM 2016)*. DEStech Publications, Lancaster, PA, 2016.

2

Semantic Technologies as Enabler

Considered a core component of business intelligence, a data warehouse deals with the management and integration of structured databases. The web has become a global data warehouse, though containing unstructured text rather than the structured content of data warehouses. Managing and integrating this huge amount of content that is intrinsically unstructured and heterogeneous in nature requires the ability to represent and store it in a manner that can be read and understood by computers and is highly scalable. Sir Tim Berners-Lee, the founder of the World Wide Web Consortium, envisioned the semantic web as a web of interconnected data, and the supporting semantic technologies made it a success. Since the introduction of linked data standards, there has been much more activity in employing semantic technologies everywhere that information is modeled. Semantic technologies can significantly improve the way we use large amounts of data. Potential benefits of semantic technologies include data integration from disparate data sources, interoperability, and efficient query answering.

2.1 Data Models

A data model defines data using high-level constructs without concerning low-level details. Various data models represent human knowledge in terms of theoretical or symbolic concepts and their relationships to make that knowledge accessible to machines such as computers for performing various tasks [Patel and Jain 2018, Jain and Mishra 2014, Rashid 2015]. Around the 1970s, all information-management systems stored their data in some hierarchical (e.g., IMS), network (e.g., CODASYL), or relational (e.g., relational database management system [RDBMS]) database [Özsu and Valduriez 2020]. With the inception of the term "expert system," where specific answers to problems are required—such as emergency response or disease diagnosis—the properties required in a database also changed dramatically:

- Data must be structured, with objects having pointers to other objects, not just flat data (strings or numbers).
- The expert-system prototypes provide an answer to a single user.
- ACID properties (atomicity, consistency, isolation, and durability) are not required in a database, because in the absence of multiple users there is no need to maintain integrity and consistency between transactions.
- Once the solution to the problem is retrieved, there is no need to store the large amount of long-lived data.
- Facts must be stored about the world.

Again, with time the expert systems started to be used across platforms and by multiple users, so they were required to exhibit ACID properties—giving rise to object-oriented databases and object-relational databases. With the rise of the Internet, databases needed to provide support for documents, hypertext, and multimedia, giving rise to Knowledge Management technologies such as content management, where the term "knowledge base" is wrongly used to refer to the repositories of documents and procedures which are meant to be understood by humans. Accurately speaking, a knowledge base is composed of facts about the world with explicit representation, commonly in the form of an ontology, that are used by the inference engine (in addition to some logic) to draw conclusions. One of the most famous knowledge-based systems was a program for medical diagnosis called MYCIN, which represented facts in a flat database and used rules to reason about them. Today, knowledge-based systems are used in many more applications than just expert systems, and the techniques used to represent knowledge bases have become more sophisticated than just assertions in a flat database. For example, frames, conceptual graphs, logical assertions, and subsumption ontology are used to represent knowledge bases in more structured formats.

With the rapid increase in semi-structured and unstructured data, it becomes important to understand all different types of data and models and tools for analyzing and managing it. Structured data conforms to a predefined schema and is the easiest to organize and search. Examples include business data like finance transactions, student grade sheets, and demographic information. A very large percentage of the data of world is unstructured data, whose elements can barely be mapped to predefined fields. Unstructured data has no structure and is therefore the most difficult to manage and analyze. Examples include multimedia data like audio, video, and images, and text documents in Microsoft Word or PDF format [Mallik et al. 2013]. Semi-structured data has some structure in it in the form of metadata or semantic tags. Examples include résumés, advertisements, text in an email, and digital photographs. While the original data is unstructured, these documents contain some metadata describing the original data.

2.1.1 Data Models for Structured Data

In the 1960s, before the advent of database models, files were used to represent machine-readable information, with records stored one per line in a text file. In the flat-file model (data level), data is stored but cannot be robustly searched and cannot represent connections or nesting. It does not allow working with a dynamic environment or extracting implicit data from the stored data. File-system descriptions could not satisfactorily solve the problem of concurrent access of data. For this reason, the file-based model vanished (approximately forty years ago), because it could not accommodate the storage of real-world entities semantically [Chihoub et al. 2020]. The only really significant surviving remnants of the flat-file database model are CSV files (comma-separated values) and Excel spreadsheets.

In the early 1970s, relational, network, and hierarchical data models (information level) were deployed, with the relational data model the most widely used for structured data even today (fifty years on) because of its simplicity and structural clarity. Hierarchical database models are used to organize data in a tree structure. Network models are an extension of hierarchical models and provide a flexible graphical representation of objects and relationships. Relational database models declaratively store data in the form of two-dimensional tables to specify data and queries. Entity-relationship models are used to describe interrelated things of interest in pictorial form, which can then be converted to the relational model—with the drawback that there is no data-manipulation language. Enhanced entity-relationship models are used to precisely reflect the constraints and properties that are found in more complex databases. While very effective at searching record content, RDBMSs are very inflexible in terms of representing arbitrary and evolving relationships between records, because of their strict adherence to tabular structure; therefore they cannot be used for cognitive knowledge-level systems, stored procedures, and binary large objects.

In the 1980s, the object-oriented paradigm provided a natural way to model semantics, and hence object-oriented databases (OODBs) emerged—although they could not live long, leaving behind their object-relational descendants. Object-oriented databases are used to represent sophisticated data and are a combination of relational (supporting tables) and object-oriented database models that directly support classes, objects, and their relationships.

2.1.2 Data Models for Semi-Structured and Unstructured Data

The persistent storage provided by a database is for well-structured and well-understood data, but real-world data is highly multimodal, encompassing an array of documents, image, videos, text, and many more unstructured facets. This highly unstructured data makes up around 80% of the world's total data. It used to be stored in data lakes and data

warehouses, and could be processed through AI and machine learning algorithms instead of being discarded.

For the exchange of this semi-structured and unstructured data, a new
metadata approach emerged. The meta-information in this approach was
represented using standard generalized markup language (SGML), which
developed to hypertext markup language (HTML) and further to eXtensible
Markup Language (XML). JSON (JavaScript Object Notation) also emerged
as an open standard and an alternative to XML for transmitting data objects.
XML and JSON documents are self-describing, with the schema elements
becoming part of data. Multimodal systems identify these implicit schema
elements and are able to query and analyze these data sets. In the mid-
2000s, NOSQL DBMSs emerged as an answer to the high cost of RDBMSs
for huge data sets and their low functionality. Driven by financial con-
siderations, ACID properties are generally relaxed for NOSQL databases,
retrograding them to the data level [Ekren and Erkollar 2020]. Some notable
NOSQL database types are wide-column databases (Cassandra), document
databases (Couchbase, MongoDB), key-value databases (Redis), and graph
databases (AllegroGraph, Neo4j, Virtuoso).

2.2 Representing Semantics

Today's systems have limitations when it comes to finding, extracting, representing, interpreting, maintaining, combining, and reusing relevant information from the large-scale distributed unstructured multimodal data
content. We require methods to derive value from the stored knowledge
and simplify the sharing and analysis of data. Semantic data models provide a way of representing and storing information while preserving its
meaning and context by virtue of relationships [Tutcher 2016]. In contrast to
traditional approaches, semantic data models encode knowledge about a
problem domain meaningfully into a machine-understandable way. Entity-
relationship diagrams, OODBs, object-relational databases, and RDF stores
are some noteworthy semantic data models [Diène et al. 2020]. Their uptake
in the semantic-web movement has provided an ample and mature set
of techniques and tool sets for implementing knowledge bases and linked-
data applications. The major characteristics of semantic models as compared to relational databases, XML schemas, and other syntax-dependent
information-exchange formats are as follows:

- **Flexibility in knowledge representation:** Semantic data models specify well-defined schemas (schema definition language) with support
  for incremental and dynamic schema evolution. In applications, new

information may arise because of de-commissioning/replacing systems, adding features, or implementing changes from external interfaces. This may require changes in the data model. Changes in syntactic data models may require expensive system modifications, versus just the addition of a few axioms in semantic data models.

- **Simple and Lightweight:** Semantic data models are simple to use and lightweight, as not all applications today require all the features of a full-fledged DBMS and heavyweight ACID properties.

- **Preservation of Meaning:** The semantics of terms in semantic data models is defined by their relationships with other terms and is stored along with the data, reducing ambiguity and preserving the intent of the information.

- **Preservation of Information:** In semantic data models, the scope of data input is not constrained to a predefined schema, but some informal or undefined extensions are possible which can be processed later.

- **Ease of system integration:** Semantic data models do not depend on any fixed schema or structure. Terms with common semantics can be queried together, and terms can be easily integrated with external resources.

- **Model Extensibility:** Semantic models can easily be extended incrementally over time, allowing new concepts and knowledge to be introduced without requiring a re-design of entire standards and systems. Semantic data models can always be extended by adding rules depending upon the context.

- **Interoperability and Expressivity:** Traditional data models can only facilitate schematic (structural) interoperability (adhering to the same data model or schema), whereas semantic data-modeling techniques are platform independent and provide some level of semantic interoperability between applications. Often in natural-language texts, multiple interpretations of one piece of data may exist. Unlike in traditional data models, terms can be disambiguated in semantic data models by considering their position and their relationships to other concepts.

2.3 Representative Semantic Data Models

Various representative semantic data models have been proposed since the 1970s [Angele et al. 2020, Tutcher et al. 2017].

2.3.1 Semantic HTML

Since its inception, HTML has been semantic by virtue of markup. Markup formats are a lightweight approach for making the web of documents machine readable and more intelligent. Markup formats use HTML markup tags to semantically annotate information items in web pages, creating an approach to tag existing web pages with machine-readable indicators for browsers and other programs to interpret. This is what today is termed POSH—plain old semantic HTML. POSH is the use of heading elements for logical outlines, table markup for making tables accessible, quotes, alt text for images, list elements, and using the tag "em" for emphasis rather than bold. This is something like separating out the content from the presentation.

The "span" and "div" elements provide more precise semantics than is expressed in HTML alone. The four most widespread formalized markup formats are microformats, microdata, RDFa, and embedded JSON-LD. Software can automatically process information intended for end users, such as products, reviews, blog posts, contact information, and calendars. As compared to explicitly codified semantics in the form of ontologies (as we will see later), markup formats are easy, because they simply embed semantic markup directly in the web page. The interoperability issue, however, remains unsolved.

Microformats were introduced around 2005 and have a fixed domain-specific vocabulary which is not extendable or customizable. But no microformats exist for some scientific data, such as chemical or zoological data. In contrast to domain-dedicated microformats, Resource Description Framework in attributes (RDFa) can be used for custom data and multiple schemas. RDFa brings the document web and the data web closer together by embedding arbitrary vocabularies into HTML if no matching microformat is found. RDFa (introduced around 2007) and JSON-LD (introduced around 2014) are World Wide Web Consortium (W3C) specifications and RDF serializations. They are therefore preferred methods of encoding. As compared to microdata, RDFa allows multiple vocabularies. JSON-LD is a lightweight and ideal linked-ata format. It organizes and connects the messy data of the web, reducing its ambiguity and uncertainty. Like JSON, JSON-LD is easy for machines to parse and generate, and it is easier for humans to read and write.

The Web Data Commons project estimates how much structured data is present on the web. It looks for various formats such as microformats, RDFa, and JSON-LD in URLs that are parsable as HTML. RDFa is common, but microdata is the format which is most used and has shown the strongest growth. When it is not clear which format should be used, a mix is always allowed. Recently, the major search engines—Google, Bing, and others—got together and created Schema.org as a vocabulary supporting markup of structured data. Schema.org seems to be more comprehensive than any of the existing markup formats; it originally used microdata, but now both microdata and RDFa are supported.

2.3.2 Using Web (2.0) APIs

Another approach is to expose some domain data and functionality by using application programming interfaces (APIs), which are interfaces for software. There are thousands of companies providing APIs across hundreds of categories. API endpoints support HTTP and are addressable over the web. The website ProgrammableWeb is the largest web API directory. There is a Linked Web APIs data set providing information about web APIs. Mashups are small, specialized applications that require data from several sources and utilize web APIs to query structured data over the web. The concept of web APIs has brought a revolution in the world of mashups. Mashup developers are required to understand the methods exposed to retrieve the data from each data set. Web APIs provide data in a structured format such as XML or JSON. This concept of web APIs has the drawback of writing an API for each data set. In addition, no standard mechanism exists for referring to something described by one API in the data that is returned by some other API. Therefore, although web APIs provide a mechanism for exposing data structurally over the web, they fail in making it linkable and hence discoverable. Here are some examples: Amazon Product Advertising API, Flickr API, and Amazon S3.

2.3.3 Publishing Linked Data

To derive insight and value from data, a move was required from the document web model to the data web model. This semantic web vision of Sir Tim Berners-Lee is scalable, versatile, and flexible [Berners-Lee and Hendler 2001]. Just as hyperlinks connect web documents, linked data connects different data sources into a single global data space by setting up links between terms of these data sources. This is the essence of linked data, which is a way to publish data globally on the web that is open, connected, and self-describing; encourages reuse; and reduces redundancy to add value to data. RDF databases (as data sources) support the use of URLs (as links) to connect to other RDF databases, thus becoming a single global data space.

Though in different encoding formats, all data sets published as linked data use the prevailing RDF data model, so no problem exists in syntactic integration. Examples include DBpedia, Wikidata, Freebase, LinkedMDB, LinkedCT, and many more. The Linked Open Data (LOD) Cloud contained 1,407 data sets as of February 2020. The data items in different data sets are effectively linked using URIs, as the RDF triples may contain URIs from different namespaces. Relational databases can be thought of as offering similar results as LOD, but with the major difference that LOD can also link those data sets, which were created without any intention of being linked together. This is because LOD uses RDF and URIs.

Google and Yahoo crawl linked data in microformats and RDFa serializations, in order to enhance their search results and other tasks. Linked data has yet to take its place within enterprises as an alternative to data warehouses, even with its advantages of pay-as-you-go data integration and a data model without schemas.

2.4 Semantic Technologies

The most indispensable requirement today is undoubtedly that a system describe concepts as well as rules semantically in a machine-understandable way. Knowledge should be represented and stored in such a way that every single piece is elucidated and specified, irrespective of the application or the domain. Semantic technologies are a set of frameworks and technologies that enable semantic data models and the data web to operate [ElDahshan et al. 2020]. Potential benefits of semantic technologies include data integration from disparate data sources, interoperability, and efficient query answering [Mishra et al. 2015, Malik et al. 2015, Mishra and Jain 2016, Pellegrini et al. 2018].

Semantic technologies are based on the solid foundation of web technologies including identifiers (URIs/IRIs), HTTP, and characters (Unicode). Then emerged various formats like XML, XHTML, Turtle, RDFa, JSON, and microformats. Standardized information-exchange data models using the RDF standard are the key to the semantic web [Euzenat and Rousset 2020]. For fine-grained data access, we have knowledge-description languages (like RDFS and OWL), query languages (like SPARQL), and rule languages (like RIF) [Jain et al. 2016, Ye et al. 2015]. Figure 2.1 depicts the complete road map of semantic technologies.

2.4.1 Foundations

The foundations of the semantic technologies stack are web technologies. We rely on all the technologies of the World Wide Web. Everything on the web (whether abstract or physical), from living through non-living to web pages, is uniquely identified by a string of characters called the Uniform Resource Identifier (URI). Unicode and URI sit on the very bottom of Figure 2.1 and form the base of semantic technologies. Unicode gives a computer number to every existing character of every written language. URI, the naming convention, has two specializations: Uniform Resource Locator (URL; a means of locating the resource on the network) and Uniform Resource Name (URN; a persistent, location-independent

Vertical axis (left, upward arrow): Effectiveness, Efficiency, Semantics, Expressiveness, Computational Complexity, Formality/Reasoning Capability

Vertical axis (inner, downward arrow): Cost of Operation, Syntactic Flexibility

Layer	1988	1990	1996	1997	1998	1999	2000	2001	2004	2005	2006	2008	2009	2010	2013	2014
Ontologies + Inference (Languages) RDFS, OWL, SPARQL, RML, RIF, SWRL						RDFS	RML	OWL	SWRL		OWL 1.1	SPARQL 1.0	OWL2		RIF	SPARQL 1.1
Data Model (Metadata) NOSQL Revolution, RDF				RDF							NOSQL					
Serializations (Standard Syntax) XML, XHTML, Turtle, RDFa, JSON, JSON-LD, Microformats			XML				XHTML, JSON		RDFa	Microformats				JSON-LD		Turtle
Foundation Technologies URI/IRI, HTTP, Unicode, HTML	Unicode	HTTP, HTML			URI					IRI						

FIGURE 2.1
Road Map of Semantic Technologies

identifier of a resource). Every URL and every URN is a URI. A URI is sufficient to retrieve a complete description of the resource on the web. A machine can unambiguously fetch RDF data (which is machine understandable), and a human can get the HTML version (which is human understandable when displayed by a browser). The International Resource Identifier (IRI) is the international variant of the URI. As compared to URIs that use only the ASCII character set, IRIs use the ISO/ Unicode universal character set [Berners-Lee et al. 2001, Shadbolt et al. 2006]. IRIs thus allow non-Latin characters like Arabic and Japanese.

2.4.2 The Data Model (RDF)

Machine-interpretable data can be exchanged in a general fashion if machines consent upon a common semantic data model. The RDF is one such core, semantic, self-describing, domain-independent, and canonical data representation format, and a generic framework for data interchange.

Given the right vocabulary, RDF provides an ingenious and simple model for representing graphs. The RDF data model can encode almost anything from conventional relational databases to all that is expressible in XML. XML is a general-purpose metalanguage, which can store data and be used for data exchange. The RDF data model[1] has an XML-like syntax, which can be serialized using various machine-readable syntaxes such as Turtle, RDF/XML, N3, and RDFa. What HTML is for the document web, RDF is for the data web. RDF data is consumable by machines and is not to be displayed on-screen for human reading.

RDF is built of statements called RDF triples, which are labeled connections between two resources. Each RDF triple is a complete and unique fact. In an RDF triple (subject, property, object), the subject and property can both be URIs and the object can be a URI or even a literal. The RDF data model is an abstract model represented as a collection of RDF triples and intrinsically representing a directed multigraph.

RDF advantages: RDF is a simple yet expressive (semantic) data model. It can be viewed as a shared vocabulary, as it refers to the unambiguous global URI of every resource used. Using this shared vocabulary is again simpler for applications. Because of the open-world assumption and RDF's ability to handle incomplete information, it provides easier and incremental data integration. RDF is a simple language with different representations: graphs that are good for human viewing, different serializations like XML and JSON that are good for machine processing, and RDF triples that are good for reasoning. With the RDF data model, different data sources can be linked together by just adding a few RDF triples, whereas in the case of an RDBMS the schema may require re-aligning and matching. The RDF data model is capable of representing unambiguously almost any kind of data in our very unpredictable world, whereas an RDBMS schema must be concise.

2.4.3 Ontology

Many researchers have given different definition over the years for three closely related words—data, information, and knowledge—but the distinction between them is not yet clear. Some authors believe that data is a representation of processing, information is a representation of informing, and knowledge is a representation of knowing; on the other side, some authors argue that data is raw material of things and information is meaningful data. We can say that data, information, and knowledge can be represented as one according to the situation. The fact that Delhi is the capital of India will be data when it is saved in a database, information when it is told to a person, and knowledge of a person who knows it.

---

[1]   https://www.w3.org/TR/rdf-primer/.

Heterogeneities of hardware and software platforms and software applications are unavoidable in any domain of study. To share data between agents in different working environments, data sets must be interoperable. The smarter connected world of today needs knowledge to be represented semantically in a well-defined and unambiguous form understandable by both human and software agents. Meaningful relationships must be exploitable within a data set. Semantic technologies can significantly improve our ability to use large amounts of data or functionalities. An information tool which permits integration and communication between different agents is an ontology, which describes and classifies knowledge. There exist different interpretations of the term; within the knowledge-engineering community, "ontology" denotes a particular entity rather than some discipline.

Ontologies constitute the core of semantic technologies, and they offer clear benefits over databases [Abaalkhail et al. 2018, Uschold and Gruninger 1996, Ra et al. 2013, Dorion et al. 2005, Smith et al. 2009]. The two most commonly used data models are relational and NOSQL. RDBMSs offer more functionality, whereas NOSQL databases are generally more time and space efficient. However, both of them need a predefined structure with only explicit information available for retrieval. It can be complicated to add new information, e.g., new entries or relations between the existing ones. Ontologies are designed to express relations, e.g., hierarchy or inheritance, in an easy and efficient way. It is possible to join or disjoin data in an ontology. Finally, they make it possible to extract implicit information using logic. This makes semantic search meaningful and facilitates ontology learning.

An ontology is an explicit specification of a conceptualization. It consists of a set of facts and a set of axioms [Malik and Jain 2020]. The set of facts describes the instances—i.e., some particular concrete situation—whereas the set of axioms describes the schema, i.e., the structure of the model. Ontology axioms are analogous to database schemas, and facts to database data.

2.4.3.1 Ontology Development

Developing an ontology is not a trivial task. Many researchers have given methods to craft/reuse and grow ontologies. The selection of a mature method is crucial. There are five main phases generally involved in the development method for every ontology: scope determination, concept identification, concept analysis and organization, encoding, and evaluation.

 a. Scope determination: This phase determines the scope of the ontology by providing an answer to the question "Why are we going to develop it?" To represent the scope of the ontology, a series of questions called competency questions can be written in consultation with the subject matter experts. The competency questions are the questions which should be answered by the knowledge base built from the domain ontology.

b. Conceptual Identification: In this phase, developers find out the concepts, the properties, and their relationships in order to present complete information in the ontology. Existing ontologies can be reused to collect the concepts.

c. Concept Analysis and Organization: The goal of this phase is to construct the hierarchy of the domain-specific information that contains concepts, properties, and their relationships.

d. Encoding: All the information of the concepts is encoded in any knowledge-description language via ontology editors.

e. Evaluation: This phase measures the quality of the ontology.

2.4.3.2 Ontology Evaluation

Ontology evaluation deals with assessing the quality and content of the ontology to ensure that the ontology is complete, accurate, clear, and concise and fulfills all criteria mentioned in Figure 2.2, whichprovides a meeting point of the criteria, aspects, approaches, and tools. The ontology is evaluated over the criteria of accuracy, adaptability, clarity, completeness, computational efficiency, conciseness, consistency, and correctness. Aspects are the various features that should be assessed, namely vocabulary, structure, representation, context, and the taxonomic and non-taxonomic relations. The approaches are the different methodologies of ontology evaluation which exist in the literature [Yew et al. 2015] including data based, human based, criteria based, logical, evolution based, task based, feature based, gold standard, and semantic approaches. Various tools exist for ontology evaluation, including OOPS!, OntoMetric, and OntoClean.

2.4.4 Knowledge-Description Languages

In traditional XML, one sentence can be represented in multiple different forms. XML does not provide a standard way to assign meaning to the represented sentence. This makes XML very unreliable and inadequate for data exchange. Semantic technologies address this issue by making available an RDF and knowledge-description languages (ontology languages) on top of it to represent semantics. Ontologies encode the knowledge about the domain under consideration and include inference rules to process the stored knowledge. Based on structure, knowledge-description languages are classified into ones based on first-order predicate logic (CycL, KIF, Common Logic), description logic (KL-ONE, Racer, Loom, OWL), and frames (OKBC, Ontolingua, OCML, F-logic).

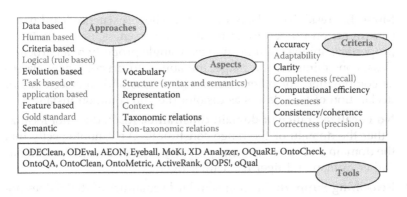

FIGURE 2.2
Ontology Evaluation (Meeting Point)

2.4.4.1 RDF Schema

The basic building block of RDF is a statement with its concrete syntax in XML. RDF provides a way of building knowledge graphs but does not constrain the graphs, because it is untyped. Stupidity is possible; nobody stops us from saying that a table eats food. RDF has no knowledge of which triples are allowed, or which thing must be the subject or object of a triple. Also, there is no assumption about a particular usage. Different people may interpret predicates subtly differently. RDF Schema (RDFS)[2] is the first step toward the "extra knowledge" that defines the vocabulary and captures the domain model semantically. It provides a language in which users can define their own classes and properties and their hierarchies. The relation between an XML schema and XML looks similar to that between RDF Schema and RDF, but differs in two major aspects. First is that the XML schema is all about validation of XML, whereas RDF Schema is about describing resources. The second difference relates to the open-world assumption of RDF Schema.

RDFS is liberal in the sense that there is no distinction between classes and individuals, and properties can themselves have properties. RDF Schema provides basic capabilities for describing taxonomies of classes and properties—i.e., RDF vocabularies—but is weak at describing resources in sufficient detail; additional capabilities have been identified as useful in an ontology language, including the following:

- **Formal Semantics:** Reasoning requires formal semantics such as class membership, consistency, equivalence of classes and individuals, classification, and semantics for containers and collections.

---

2   https://www.w3.org/TR/rdf-schema/.

- **More Expressivity:** RDFS does not allow existence/cardinality constraints on properties; transitivity, inverseness, or symmetry of properties; unique identification by a single property of a particular class; constraints on the range; the ability to describe new classes as combinations of other classes via unions and intersections; or declaration of two classes as disjoint (i.e., no common instance).

- **No Localized range or domain constraints:** RDFS does not localize either the domain or the range constraints. We cannot specify that the domain and range of some property are same—e.g., human has Father human and tiger has Father tiger.

- **Reasoning Support:** The non-standard semantics of RDFS does not have reasoning support.

2.4.4.2 Web Ontology Language

RDFS has some limitations in terms of representation and semantics, so Web Ontology Language (OWL) was built on top of it to overcome some of them. OWL is a family of highly expressive modeling languages for authoring ontologies for the data web. It provides a far larger vocabulary than RDFS (set operations; transitive, symmetric, functional, or inverse properties; equivalence; disjointness; restrictions; and much more) in addition to doing all that RDFS can do. OWL imposes a more rigid structure than RDFS does; in contrast, RDFS allows us any triple we want. OWL is an ideal modeling language: it allows for the discovery of new triples, i.e., performing inference or generating new relationships among data based on a set of rules.

OWL too suffers from some very serious challenges that limit its practical applicability [Mishra et al. 2019]. Thus came OWL 2, another W3C recommendation. There isn't just one OWL standard, though; instead, there are different flavors (also called profiles or species) corresponding to different usage models: OWL 2/Full, OWL 2/QL, OWL 2/EL, OWL 2/RL, and inoperative OWL versions (OWL/Full, OWL/DL, and OWL/Lite). Each profile of OWL is a simpler and distinct subset of the full OWL standard. With all the different flavors in existence, a trade-off is made between computational efficiency and expressive modeling power while performing reasoning. OWL 2/Full is the most expressive profile, if no reasoning is required.

2.4.4.3 Simple Knowledge Organization System

Organizations require sharing simple knowledge bases (thesauruses, taxonomies, classification schemes, subject headings, vocabularies, or any other structured controlled vocabulary) for common tasks. We need specifications to represent, access, and navigate them [Ait-Ameur et al. 2017, Kumar et al.

2019]. Simple Knowledge Organization System (SKOS) is a common data model for organizing and expressing knowledge in a machine-readable manner that can then be processed by computers and exchanged between computer applications. The SKOS data model is defined as an OWL ontology, with its data expressed as RDF triples.

2.4.5 Serializations (Syntax/Formats)

Serialization is how a graph is represented in textual form so that machines can automatically parse content into its elementary constituents. For this, we require syntaxes with formally defined grammars. As already stated, RDF is a system of identifiers, syntax, and semantics for encoding and decoding information. It is an abstract language with the ability to create sentences and statements for RDF documents using a variety of notations (machine-readable serialization formats), including existing generic syntaxes like JSON and XML and custom syntaxes like RDF/XML, Notation3 (N3), Turtle, and N-Triples.

- RDF/XML: The oldest and best-known syntactic representation of RDF defined by the W3C. The weird mixture of a treelike XML document and a triple-based RDF graph makes RDF/XML conceptually difficult, but it has the advantage of reusing existing XML tools for syntax validation and transformation. RDF/XML does not really reflect the triple model, so it is best used when one really needs to work with XML.

- RDF/JSON: JavaScript object notation (JSON) is a representational format composed of simple syntactic structures (string, array, hash). It serializes the set of RDF triples for an RDF graph as a series of syntactic and nested data structures. It is based on JavaScript, making it easy for web programmers to understand. JSON-LD is the newest specification; JSON is deprecated unless specifically necessary.

- Notation3 (.n3): More closely resembles the RDF triple model than does RDF/XML. It is a shorthand non-XML serialization of the RDF data model and is much more compact and human understandable than RDF/XML notation. N3 is very complex and also supports RDF rules, and hence is costlier and harder to parse.

- Turtle (.ttl): Terse RDF Triple Language (Turtle) is a more popular, very similar successor to N3. It is used when the reasoning or rules of N3 is not required and the RDF must be manually read and edited. It is still a more human understandable and compact syntax than N3. Turtle syntax uses "@prefix" to define the prefix and later on uses just qualified names. It uses the abbreviated form of triples with semantic sugar (semicolon and comma). Though a bit simpler to parse than N3, Turtle is still quite costly to parse as compared to N-Triples, another successor of N3.

- N-Triples (.nt): A further proper subset of Turtle, which in turn is the simplified version of N3. N-Triples is a simple textual serialization for encoding an RDF graph. It disallows Turtle shortcuts, @prefixes, and any other fancy features, and requires that all RDF terms (including URLs) be written in their full form. This makes N-Triples trivial to parse but wastes precious bandwidth. N-Triples is mainly used when good machine-to-machine communication is required. The lack of @prefixes and shorthand makes the text a bit lengthy and tough for human consumption.

- RDFa: Provides semantic context to the content of web pages by adding attributes to (X)HTML elements, thus avoiding the need to have a separate document for metadata. It makes HTML documents a bit larger, and parsing them becomes a bit more complicated and costly than parsing an RDF-only format like N-Triples. RDFa is used when existing HTML pages need to be extended with semantics.

- JSON-LD: An extension of JSON, and not specific to RDF. JSON-LD has lots of features to make it more readable to humans, thus making it more verbose. Composed of a very simple structure, JSON does have inherent meaning. JSON-LD leverages this and adds all that is missing in JSON while still taking advantage of its syntactic simplicity. JSON-LD is both a JSON document and an RDF document. It is used to improve an existing JSON API. Though most serialization formats represent an RDF graph in a treelike structure made up of RDF triples, JSON-LD represents it as a graph. Other multiple-graph formats are also available today, like TriG and N-Quads. N-Quads is similar to N-Triples but supports multiple graphs. TriG is an extension of Turtle.

2.4.6 Manipulating RDF Data

Having RDF data available is not enough. Once specified with the RDF data model for better computer understanding, knowledge must be stored and accessed by applications. We need tools to store the RDF data and schema and process, transform, and reason with it—i.e., a way to interact with the RDF model. A semantic repository comprises a store for RDF data together with middleware. The RDF store can be main memory, files, or even a database. The access methods should transparently access the data. There is a layer called RDF middleware which implements seamless access to the RDF data from the data store. This RDF middleware provides methods for querying, adding, deleting, and exporting data and providing inference over it.

2.5 RDF Data Access and Management

Querying and inference—i.e., providing access to applications—is the very purpose of representing information in a machine-accessible way.

2.5.1 RDF Data Storage

Relational databases are a rigid, structured, and well-established methodology for storing structured data, as compared to their NOSQL counterparts, which are document oriented. NOSQL graph databases store and manage data that is represented as an unlabeled or undirected or weighted graph. An RDF database is a specialized database for RDF triples, also called a triple store. Triple stores are a type of NOSQL graph store that store a special directed labeled graph, i.e., an RDF graph. Triple stores also use URIs required for querying and reasoning. They offer several advantages compared to traditional RDBMSs:

Schema Flexibility: The schema does not have to be defined in advance, making alteration of the data model easy; the schema can be changed on the fly without any redesign. Artificial tables are not required to specify the many-to-many relationships.

Standardization: All triple stores speak the same language—i.e., RDF—which has standard serialization formats like N-Triples and N-Quads. RDF is not specific to a vendor; RDF data can be moved, imported, and exported between different stores.

Efficient Querying: SPARQL is highly standardized as compared to SQL. Querying with SQL becomes inefficient, complex, and complicated at times. SPARQL provides a better level of trust and provenance.

Less Costly and Less Time Consuming: RDF triple stores are capable of querying diverse data that is evolving and comes from different data sources. This makes these storage solutions more cost-efficient and less time consuming than SQL databases.

Easy Sharing: The use of URIs makes data sharing in triple stores very simple.

Relationship Discovery: Triple stores uncover hidden implicit facts and relationships out of the original explicit data. By handling large amounts of data, triple stores improve the knowledge-handling capabilities of an organization.

Different Methods of RDF Data Storage: As the number of applications and schema-less data sets has increased, so has the need to efficiently store them. A complete triple store can be viewed as a relational table with three columns: the subject, the property, and the object. This single-table method has several drawbacks, such as the fact that all interesting queries will require many self-joins over the RDF table. With an increase in the number of triples, the execution time of queries is also increased, and due to memory consumption, more indexes are required. Inference at assertion time is infeasible as the number of triples scales, since for each entailment rule many more triples are stored. So let us study different methods of RDF storage. For small data sets with a few triples, we can use an RDF file published on the web or stored locally (e.g., .rdf, .nt, .ttl, .n3). For large data sets with thousands to millions of triples, database solutions are better. The data is stored in a database usually in the form of RDF storage. For legacy data, it is advisable to keep it in its original form and provide mapping to RDF, i.e., expose it to the outer world as RDF. RDF data management systems can be classified broadly into three categories: in-memory, non-native, and native stores.

- **In-Memory Stores:** In-memory RDF stores have transient—i.e., temporary—storage of triples in main memory. Main-memory storage techniques are obviously the fastest, but they are time consuming during the loading and parsing of RDF files and during the creation of indexes. Examples of in-memory native RDF data stores include Hexastore, Bitmat, Sesame-Memory, and Jena-Memory.

- **Non-Native Stores:** Non-native stores have persistent storage of RDF triples on top of different relational databases. They are web-based approaches including GRDDL (Gleaning Resource Descriptions from Dialects of Languages), microformat, and RSS (Really Simple Syndication) feeds, among others. Relational databases are well established to store information, and they provide query support in the form of SQL. Non-native storage solutions have the drawback that RDF data stored in an RDBMS is difficult to query: the query mechanism is represented by a series of join instructions. Non-native solutions are preferred when there are many updates or when good concurrency control is needed. Examples include Jena SDB using MySQL or Postgres, Sesame-DB, IBM Db2, and OpenLink Virtuoso.

- **Native Stores:** Native stores have persistent storage of RDF triples with their self-storage implementation, also called purpose-built frameworks. They can make use of well-known index structures such as B-trees. The time required to provide a response to a query is occasionally unacceptable because of disk-based access. The persistent storage is further distinguished as either stand-alone or embedded representations. Stand-alone disk-based RDF data stores include N3, N-Triples, Turtle, and RDF/XML. Embedded disk-based RDF data stores include RDFa, eRDF (embedded RDF), and SMW (Semantic MediaWiki). Native solutions are fast, scalable, and the most popular for RDF stores. Examples include Jena TDB, Sesame Native, Kowari, YARS, AllegroGraph, Oracle 11g, Bigdata, 4store, Stardog, GraphDB, and Urika.

Non-native storage techniques are not RDF data-model compliant, as opposed to their native counterparts. Usually non-native stores make a mapping onto a DBMS and then use some indexing in this field, whereas the indexing schemes used by native stores are closer to the RDF data model. The RDF data and schema can be manipulated efficiently in main memory, whereas for persistent storage it has to be first serialized to files. In spite of all this, non-native storage is more reasonable than its native counterparts for very large amounts of data. A fourth category of triple stores has recently come under investigation as possible storage managers for RDF. They are the NOSQL triple stores. For example, CumulusRDF is a NOSQL triple store using Apache Cassandra for the back end and Sesame for to provide SPARQL query facility. Another example is Jena+HBase, which uses Apache HBase for the back end and Jena to provide SPARQL query facility

2.5.2 Query Processing

Querying has been discussed at W3C since 1998. Accessing knowledge and querying it is the very purpose of representing knowledge in a machine-understandable way. A query language allows a user to query a data source (a relational database, the web, an XML file, or even a simple text file) to retrieve information. Some types of query languages are those for RDBMSs (SQL), those for XML data sources (XPointer, XQuery, XPath), those for RDF graphs (SPARQL), and those for RDF in Jena models (RDQL). A multiple indexing framework is utilized for the RDF data model, where all three RDF items—i.e., subject (s), property (p), and object (o)—are paid equal attention. In this framework, a set of six indexes is maintained that covers all possible access schemes. For querying an RDF store, two approaches are mainly used: using a proprietary API and using a query language. Proprietary query APIs define their own query format, like DLDB, KAON, Query, and SeRQL. For querying RDF documents, the query languages available include SQL-like ones (RQL, SeRQL, RDQL, SPARQL), language-like ones (Metalog), XPath-like ones (Versa, RDFPath), rules-like ones (Triple, OWL-QL), and XML languages (XSLT, XQuery). Out of all these styles, by far most the popular are SQL-like query languages. Querying RDF is quite different from querying an XML document for the following three major reasons:

- An XML document is a document tree, whereas an RDF graph is a set of triples.
- The atomic units of XML and RDF are different: XML has elements, attributes, and text, whereas RDF has triples, URIs, blank nodes, and text.
- The description language for XML is DTD or an XML schema, whereas for RDF it is RDF Schema.

Because of these differences, a query framed for an RDF graph has to be different from an XML query. XML query solutions do not entirely fit RDF. Also, the ongoing research on context and named graphs does not fit all query languages. RDF data stores and RDFS and OWL ontologies based on the RDF data model can be best queried using their own query language, in the same manner as relational databases are queried using SQL.

SPARQL (SPARQL Protocol and RDF Query Language): SPARQL is the current W3C recommendation for querying RDF data [Galgonek et al. 2016]. It is a query language as well as a protocol for conveying SPARQL queries from query clients to query processors. Though many RDF query languages even more expressive than SPARQL are available and have existed longer than it, they are not supported by most of the available tools, which hinders interoperability. SPARQL is based on RDQL. The query types include select, construct, ask, and describe. SPARQL allows definition of prefixes for namespaces. The SPARQL query language is based on matching graph patterns against RDF graphs. It has a rich set of operators and functions. Between SPARQL and the RDF data store lies a layer (e.g., SAIL in Sesame) that takes care of translating the parsed query into an actual storage-compliant query.

EXAMPLE: If we want to fetch all the relationships of the subject "s" in Jena, it looks like this:
StmtIterator iter=model.listStatements(s,null,null);
while(iter.hasNext())
    {
st = iter.next();
p = st.getProperty();
o = st.getObject();
do_something(p,o);
    }

In SPARQL, it looks like this:
SELECT?p?o
WHERE {s?p?o}\

2.5.2.1 Adding, Deleting, and Exporting Data

An API is used to create new concepts, properties, or instances in the main memory and then to store them in the RDF store. Alternatively, the complete ontology is loaded into the main memory; RDF statements are then read using a parser and mapped on an object model. An RDF validator may be used to check the read data from the ontology for correctness and compliance with the schemas already loaded. Completely deleting all the instances from the RDF store is simple, whereas deleting single instances calls for the utmost care, as it could entail the deletion of other related statements. For exporting data to other systems, various serialization formats exist (discussed earlier).

SPARQL 1.1 provides languages and a protocol to facilitate querying as well as accessing RDF graph content in an RDF store or on the web. Different query result formats, including XML, JSON, and CSV, are supported by SPARQL 1.1.

2.5.3 Inference/Reasoning

By inference/reasoning we mean deriving facts and relationships that are not explicit in the knowledge base based on the asserted information and some additional information (perhaps vocabularies or rules). Two terms are used to refer to the same concept, namely inference (when new facts are inferred from the existing ones) and reasoning (when some agent, either human or machine, reasons over or questions a data set) [Dentler et al. 2011, Haarslev et al. 2012]. In this book, both terms have been used interchangeably. Inference improves the quality of data integration by discovering new relationships and possible inconsistencies. Inferencing within the knowledge bases represented using RDFS and OWL languages is based on the constructs and semantics defined in those languages.

2.5.3.1 *Ontology Reasoning*

Ontology reasoning (OWL reasoning or DL reasoning) aims to provide tools and services to ontology users. It mostly utilizes first-order logic and proceeds through strategies of forward and backward chaining. Basic DL reasoning problems include concept satisfiability, concept subsumption, consistency of ABox with respect to TBox, and realization and retrieval of individuals. Ontology reasoning is utilized mainly to maintain high-quality ontologies with detailed descriptions which are meaningful, non-redundant, and correct; answer various queries over the concepts and instances of the ontology, like finding superclasses and subclasses and retrieving instances matching a given query; and align and merge multiple ontologies.

For the sake of simplicity, in this book a DL reasoner is treated the same as an OWL reasoner. Various automated DL reasoners exist, ranging from open source (FaCT++, Pellet, Racer, HermiT) through closed source (Cyc, KAON2) to commercial ones (Bossam, RacerPro, OntoBroker). The kind of reasoning that these DL reasoners perform is confined to the semantics and expressivity that the knowledge-description language provides. OWL has some limitations when it comes to modeling complex relationships that are beyond the normal expressivity of OWL. This limits the kind of inferences that they can participate in. The solution to this is to combine ontologies and rules.

2.5.3.2 Rule-Based Reasoning

Intelligent manipulation and exploitation of information may not always be possible by DL reasoning. To support complete knowledge-based services and ontology reasoning, rule-based reasoning is required. DL reasoning engines have low performance at ABox reasoning and querying. By use of rules, arbitrary integrity constraints can be defined over the ABox. We can state expressive queries on individuals by combining DL reasoners and the rule paradigm, thus increasing performance. Moreover, DL reasoners work on the open-world assumption and are committed to monotonicity. Sometimes it is preferable—even required—to introduce some non-monotonicity in DL reasoners, for, e.g., negation as failure.

Businesses and business applications use rules in every aspect of their decision-making process. We have standard rule representation and reasoning techniques for use in business, diagnosis, the semantic web, legal reasoning, access authentication, web services, and other web (as web 2.0) areas. Rules are a common form of procedural knowledge but encoded in a declarative format. They overcome the expressive limitations of knowledge representation formalisms.

2.6 Rules and Rule Languages

A rule is a statement in the general form "if condition, then action," containing clauses combined through logical operators. Rules are projected to support ontologies for efficient domain knowledge representation. Many parts of a business are not naturally modeled with OWL. To enhance the expressivity of OWL and model more domain knowledge, a rule language can be used [Mehla and Jain 2019, Hewahi 2018, Rattanasawad et al. 2013].

2.6.1 Kinds of Rules

Rules can be divided into four categories:

- **Deductive Rules:** Also termed derivation or deduction or constructive rules, deductive rules derive new implicit knowledge by using logical inference over the existing explicit knowledge. Deductive rules take the form "head ← body." If the body part matches to some fact in the underlying knowledge bases, the data of the head part is immediately inferred. The head and the body parts of the rule usually share variables (?x). An example of a deductive rule is "If age of ?x greater than 18 Then ?x is adult." The "if" part of the rule is called the body, and the "then" part the head. In this example, both the head and body parts have the common variable x, which is replaced by a person. The "construct" clause of SPARQL query language can be viewed as a deductive rule, as it deduces new RDF triples from existing RDF data sets. Most logical rule languages are based on the concept of deductive rules, like Prolog, Xcerpt, SQL views in databases, and Datalog.

- **Normative Rules:** Also termed structural rules or integrity constraints, normative rules pose constraints on the data values or logic of an application instead of inferring new knowledge. Such rules prevent inconsistencies from happening in the knowledge base. The classical example is an integrity constraint in an RDBMS, e.g., every student has a roll number which is unique. Other examples are cardinality restrictions and primary and foreign key constraints.

- **Reactive Rules:** Also termed reaction or active or dynamic or event-condition-action (ECA) rules, reactive rules respond to the occurrence of specific events by automatically executing a specified action. These rules are generally recognized as being of two types: ECA and production rules. ECA rules are rules of the form "ON event IF condition DO action," which specifies that if the condition holds, the action should be taken automatically upon the detection of the event. The event can be an atomic event or a composite one. The action can be an update of data, changes to the rule set, a procedure call, or even another event to be triggered. An example of an ECA rule is "ON request from parent of ?x IF ?x is eligible DO admit ?x to school." Production rules take the form "IF condition THEN action." The condition statement of a production rule continuously queries the working memory. Whenever the condition is true, the action is executed.

2.6.2 Rule Languages

Representation of rules has been standardized using rule markup languages that allow rule sharing between business applications. They allow rules to be published, exchanged, transferred, interchanged, and integrated, and enable rule-language interoperability and expressivity. In general, rule markup languages come in two different syntaxes: XML-based syntax that is used by machines, and human-readable syntax. RuleML has been around a while. Rule Interchange Format (RIF) formalizes the patterns and formats required to communicate rules among different systems. The five most widely used rule languages are FOL RuleML, W3C RIF, Notation3, SWRL, and Jena. Each rule language supports various functions and concepts and has its own syntactic and semantic peculiarities.

- **RuleML (Rule Markup Language)** is based on XML. It expresses both forward and backward rules in XML. All rule types are supported by RuleML, which focuses on the interoperation of rules and can be used for "queries and inferences in Web ontologies, mappings between Web ontologies, and dynamic Web behaviors of workflows, services, and agents."[3]

- **SWRL (Semantic Web Rule Language)**[4] is a rule language submitted for recommendation to W3C in 2004. It is intended to be the rule language of the semantic web. SWRL extends OWL 2/DL with Horn-clause rules (a subset of RuleML) and augments the declarative expressivity of OWL ontologies—but at the expense of decidability. All rules are expressed in terms of OWL concepts and are saved as part of the ontology. Applying SWRL rules in an ontology is much easier, because of the simplicity it offers. Most of the inference engines, such as Pellet and HermiT, provide support for SWRL. SWRL is monotonic (counting, negated atoms, and retraction are not supported). The high-level abstract syntax of SWRL is supported by many tools, including Protégé, KAON2, and RacerPro. The following are examples of SWRL rules:
Person(?p) $\wedge$ hasSibling(?p,?s) $\wedge$ Man(?s) $\Rightarrow$ hasBrother(?p,?s)
hasParent(?x,?y) $\wedge$ hasBrother(?y,?z) $\Rightarrow$ hasUncle(?x,?z)

- **RIF (Rule Interchange Format):** The RIF W3C working group was chartered in late 2005 to produce a core rule language plus extensions as a set of dialects to enable the exchange of rules among different rule systems. One single language may not satisfy the needs of many popular business modeling rule paradigms, so RIF is meant to provide semantics that preserve mapping from one rule system to another. The idea of RIF is to provide mechanisms for rule systems to be able to map rules in their native language to RIF and back. This idea presents a standard method for rule translation and sharing. RIF is a more expressive language than SWRL, and reached final recommendation in 2010.[5]

- **R2ML (REWERSE Rule Markup Language)** is based on the concept of SWRL, RuleML, and Object Constraint Language (OCL). It supports derivation, integrity constraints, production, and reaction (ECA) rules. R2ML aims at providing an XML rule format for rule translation without information loss, facilitating ontologies to have rules and tools for visualization of rule systems.[6]

- **Jena Rules:** The Jena RDF/OWL library contains support for both forward- and backward-chaining rules. Jena Rules follow the

---
[3] http://ruleml.org/.
[4] https://www.w3.org/Submission/SWRL/.
[5] https://www.w3.org/2005/rules/wg/charter.html.
[6] https://www.w3.org/2005/rules/wg/wiki/R2ML.

syntax "[ruleName: antecedents -> consequent]," with the ante-cedents expressed as triple patterns. Jena2 is much simpler, as it allows rules to be represented in a very compact form in text source files.[7]

- **OWL 2/RL:** Since DLs and Horn logic are orthogonal, not ev-erything in DL can be expressed using rules. So a subset of OWL DL must be found, so that OWL constructs can be mapped to logic programming. OWL 2/RL is one such profile of OWL 2. It is the intersection of DL and Horn logic. Expressivity can be implemented using either forward- or backward-chaining rule engines. OWL 2/RL has the drawback of restricted expressivity.[8]

- **Notation3:** N3 rules rely on N3 syntax for graphs. They are not widely implemented.[9]

2.6.2.1 Discussion

RuleML is an XML approach for representing rules. RIF is a W3C standard for exchanging. The rule language SWRL is not bound to any execution algorithm; in contrast, other rule languages are generally tied to the Rete algorithm; providing many benefits to SWRL. SWRL has freedom in choosing the evaluation algorithm and changing it at any time without af-fecting the business rules. As compared to SWRL, rules written in other engines often have side effects. The rule author needs to prioritize the rules and be aware of the algorithm that is used to execute them. SWRL is in-tegrated tightly with OWL, meaning that there is no mismatch between the modeling language and the rules language.

2.7 Semantic Tools

In the last few years, semantic tools have greatly increased. They provide an interface to carry out some major activities of semantic techniques.

2.7.1 Ontology Development Environments

Ontology development environments are the editors, browsers, and in-tegrated suites that can be used for building a new ontology from scratch or for reusing and growing already-existing ontologies. The first-ever ontology

---

[7] https://jena.apache.org/documentation/inference/#rules.
[8] https://www.w3.org/TR/rif-owl-rl/.
[9] https://www.w3.org/2004/12/rules-ws/paper/94/.

development tool, Ontolingua Server, appeared in the mid-1990s. Today various tools are available, such as TopBraid Composer, Swoop, Protégé, OWLGrED, NeOn Toolkit, Neologism, Vitro, Knoodl, Anzo for Excel, Fluent Editor, Semantic Turkey, VocBench, WebOnto, Ontosaurus, and OntoEdit. Among all available ontology development tools, Protégé is the most predominantly used because of various plug-ins that help in building an intelligent system.

2.7.2 RDF-izers

Most of the world's data today is in non-RDF format. RDF-izers provide a bridge between the document web and the data web by providing a middleware service of converting virtually any data record with varying formats or serializations into RDF data-model serializations. RDF-izers are also called converters, translators, or spongers.

a. Triplify is a lightweight plug-in for web applications written in PHP for converting database content into RDF, JSON, or linked data.[10]

b. D2RQ provides access to relational databases as RDF graphs. It is open source and provides RDF-based access to databases but does not require replicating the contents as an RDF store. It supports many databases including MySQL, Oracle, SQL Server, and PostgreSQL.[11]

c. The RDB2RDF Working Group at W3C also provides mapping of data in relational tables and relational schemas into RDF and OWL.[12]

2.7.3 Application Programming Interfaces

These are the frameworks or programming tool kits that provide functionality for storage, querying, and inference over RDF data. Program API libraries are available for most programming libraries, e.g., Jena, Sesame, and RDFSuite for Java; Redland for C; and RDFStore for Perl.

2.7.3.1 Apache Jena

Jena is a Java-based free and open-source framework for dealing with linked data scenarios. It provides a Java library that allows manipulation (storage, query, and inference) of RDF graphs. It is composed of several

---

[10] http://triplify.org.
[11] http://d2rq.org/.
[12] http://www.w3.org/2001/sw/rdb2rdf/.

APIs and command-line tools. The allowed data serializations are RDF/ XML, Turtle, and Notation3. Apache Jena also includes a SPARQL server, Apache Jena Fuseki, which can be run as a stand-alone server. It offers access to the same Jena features using a HTTP interface. The Jena API is language neutral and provides a consistent programming interface irrespective of the ontology language used. It provides an intensive set of Java libraries to develop Java code to work with RDF-based ontologies and rules.

- Storage: Jena supports different ways of storing RDF statements: in memory, in plain files, and in an RDBMS. Apache Jena SDB of the Jena semantic web framework is a persistent storage using conventional relational databases. Many open-source and proprietary databases are supported. Apache Jena TDB is another component of the Jena semantic web framework and is faster, more scalable, and better supported than SDB.

- Query: It supports RDQL and SPARQL for retrieving information from graphs.

- Reasoning: Jena has built-in RDF-S and OWL reasoning support, and also a built-in rule engine implemented in Java. Developers can add customized reasoning rules. Jena allows both Rete-style forward chaining and tabled SLG resolution-based backward chaining. It has its own rule language and built-in rule engine implemented in Java for the evaluation of rules on top of RDF. It is the most complex and integrated, though sophisticate, rule system. The user can add customized rules. Jena provides many reasoners: a transitive reasoner, an RDFS rule reasoner, an OWL reasoner, and a generic rule reasoner.[13]

2.7.3.2 *Eclipse RDF4J (Formerly OpenRDF Sesame)*

RDF4J (Sesame) is an official fork of the OpenRDF Sesame project. OpenRDF Sesame is a Java-based open-source framework for storage, inference, and querying of RDF and RDF Schema. It can be used as a standalone server—i.e., a database for RDF and RDF Schema—and also as a Java library. Sesame is a lightweight yet powerful API with reasoning and transactional support.

- Storage: Eclipse RDF4J, or Sesame, is an open-source, database-independent storage for RDF data. It can be combined with a variety of DBMSs like MySQL, PostgreSQL, or Oracle 9i or newer. In its architecture it contains a layer named SAIL (Storage and

---

[13] http://jena.sourceforge.net.

Inference Layer) for managing communication with the database in use. It provides support for all three types of storage: in-memory and native data stores and APIs for integrating with RDF databases.

- Query: Sesame can accept only queries written in SeRQL (an RDF query language) and converts them into queries suitable to run on the underlying repository.

- Reasoning: It does not have any support for OWL, so it is not suitable for ontologies.[14]

2.7.3.3 Redland C Libraries

The Redland RDF framework is a framework of free, object-based, modular C libraries and APIs that provide support for manipulating RDF. Redland provides a parser for different serializations of RDF like RDF/XML, Turtle, and N-Triples, and interfaces to languages like C#, Perl, Python, Objective-C, Ruby, PHP, Java, and Tcl via the Redland bindings package. Many projects use these libraries, including the FOAF Explorer, OWL Mindswap, and Amaya.

- Storage: APIs are available for storage in memory and also persistently with multiple databases.

- Query: Redland can accept queries written in SPARQL and RDQL, as well as GRDDL implementation for the web.[15]

2.7.3.4 OWL API

OWL API is a free and open-source Java framework for creating, manipulating, and serializing OWL 2 ontologies. It is created and maintained by the University of Manchester (UK). It includes a parser and writers for serializing ontologies in syntaxes like RDF/XML, OWL/XML, Turtle, OBO, and more. It also includes APIs for interfacing to various reasoners and validators for the various OWL 2 profiles. OWL API is OWL-centric, meaning that representation of class expressions and axioms is not at the level of RDF triples.

- Reasoning: OWL API provides the OWLReasoner to interface with the OWL reasoners. Many reasoners are supported via this API, including FaCT++, HermiT, Pellet, TrOWL, ELK, and Snorocket.[16]

---

[14] https://rdf4j.org/.
[15] http://librdf.org/.
[16] http://owlcs.github.io/owlapi.

2.7.3.5 Sparta

Sparta is a Python API for RDF by Mark Nottingham. It is designed to easily navigate the semantic web programmatically.[17]

2.7.3.6 Protégé-OWL API

Protégé is a Java-based, open-source, and freely available ontology editor tool and API for RDFS and OWL by Stanford University. It has a plug-in architecture allowing for a number of semantic tools. It has an OWL plug-in for editing RDF and OWL ontologies and SWRL rules, as well as the OWLViz visual editor for OWL ontologies. WebProtégé, an extended version of Protégé, is also free and open source. WebProtégé takes the functionality of Protégé to the web for editing OWL 2 ontologies.

- Storage: Protégé provides storage back ends to Sesame and Jena.
- Query: The Protégé-OWL API provides methods for querying and manipulating OWL models.
- Reasoning: The reasoning is performed using DL engines.

Though Apache Jena doesn't support full OWL 2, RDF triples can still be added to build OWL constructs—but this must be hand coded without API support. Alternatively, OWL API can be used, taking care of writing OWL axioms as opposed to RDF triples.

2.7.4 Semantic Repository and Reasoner

A semantic repository allows efficient storage of RDF data as well as schema information. It also includes a reasoner to access (query and inference) the stored information. A semantic reasoner is also called a triple store, an RDF store, an RDF database, an RDF repository, metastore, or a knowledge base [Banane and Belangour 2019]. It has two primary components, namely the repository to store the information and the middleware that builds on top of that repository to provide methods for adding, deleting, querying, and exporting that information. In this way, a semantic repository combines the features of both a DBMS and an inference engine. Some semantic repositories have already been discussed in the text, such as Apache Jena and Sesame; the rest are discussed here.

---

[17] https://github.com/mnot/sparta/.

- **Oracle Spatial and Graph** is a W3C standards-based graph store in Oracle Database for knowledge graph, linked data, and social network applications.[18]
- **RDFLib** is a pure Python package working with RDF for in-memory storage and persistent storage on top of Berkeley DB.[19]
- **Virtuoso:** Virtuoso Universal Server is another alternative for implementing triple stores. It can access RDF data stored in an RDBMS repository, which may be part of Virtuoso itself or external. The usual database schema is relatively simple: RDF data are stored as quads in a table with four columns. A quad includes the triple of subject s, predicate p, and object o plus graph name G. Regarding the query language, Virtuoso uses a combination of SPARQL and SQL. It translates SPARQL queries to SQL according to the database schema.
- **AllegroGraph** is a commercial RDF graph database and application framework developed by Franz Inc. based on Common Lisp. There are different editions of AllegroGraph and different clients. AllegroGraph enables linked data applications through a graph database and an application framework. It offers similar features as the other tools described here: storing and retrieving triple data. It allows access from Python, Java, and Ruby, and queries in SPARQL. It supports data serializations like RDF/XML, Turtle, N-Triples, N-Quads, TriX, and TriG formats, and it can be used with various programming languages. Similar to a relational database, it supports ACID transactions.[20]
- **4store:** 4store is an RDF DBMS which stores RDF data as quads, adding an additional property for storing the graph name. 4store uses a custom data structure for storing the quads and uses its own 4s-query tool for querying them.[21]
- **GraphDB (formerly OWLIM)** is a triple store by Ontotext with a GNU Lesser General Public License and a commercial licence. It is a Java-based semantic repository that provides inductive, scalable, and lightweight reasoning over a pragmatic subset of OWL. It comes in three different editions: Lite, Standard, and Enterprise. GraphDB is packaged as a SAIL for the Sesame OpenRDF framework. It is based on TRREE (Triple Reasoning and Rule Entailment Engine).[22]

---

[18] https://www.oracle.com/database/technologies/spatialandgraph/rdf-graph-features.html.
[19] https://rdflib.readthedocs.org/en/latest/.
[20] https://franz.com/agraph/allegrograph/.
[21] https://4store.github.io/.
[22] http://graphdb.ontotext.com/.

- **Stardog** is an enterprise, Java-based, proprietary platform built on smart graph technology. It supports all of the OWL 2 profiles.[23]
- **Mulgara** is an open-source, Java-based RDF database for storage and retrieval of RDF-based metadata.[24]

2.7.5 Semantic Reasoner

A semantic reasoner is a piece of software that is used to deduce new facts from unambiguously stated facts or asserted axioms. Reasoners can also be utilized to check the logical consistency of the ontology model. There are reasoners for all the OWL species. A typical rule engine contains an inference engine, a rule base, and a fact base (working memory). The inference engine finds the combination of facts from the working memory that satisfies rules to decide which rules to activate and finally fire (execute). There are various rule-language families. Instances in a family may differ in their syntax, semantics, or other aspects.

The term "reasoner" generally means an OWL reasoner or an ontology reasoner, and may not have rule support at all, with everything being operated just with facts and axioms. On the other hand, rule engines like Drools, CLIPS, and Jess are self-contained and more expressive than OWL reasoners. All these rule engines provide APIs for ontology reasoning also. But these rule engines are slow, as the user has the freedom to write the rules, and require special setup. For example, Drools has Drools-SWRLAPI and Jess has SWRL API for OWL reasoning. Some ontology reasoners also provide support for rule reasoning; Pellet provides support for SWRL. FaCT++ does not support rules at all.

Many APIs and integrated development environments for RDF provide support for ontology reasoners as well as rule engines. For example, Protégé provides access to RacerPro through the RacerProTG plug-in, SWRL through SWRLTab, and the Jess rules engine through JessTab, HermiT, Pellet, and FaCT++. The Apache Jena framework also provides a range of reasoners, including the OWL reasoner, the RDFS rule reasoner, and a generic rule reasoner.

Ontology reasoners include the following:

OWL DL: Pellet (Java based, open source), HermiT (Java based), Fast Classification of Terminologies (FaCT++; C++, open source), Renamed ABoxes and Concept Expression Reasoner (RacerPro)

OWL EL: ELK (Java based, open source), CEL (Lisp based, open source), SHER, Snorocket (Java based), ELLY (extension of IRIS)

OWL RL: OWLIM, Jena (Java based, HP Labs), ELLY, Oracle OWL Reasoner (part of 11g), BaseVISor (Java based)

---

[23] http://stardog.com/.
[24] http://www.mulgara.org/.

OWL QL: OWLIM, Owlgres (open source), QuOnto, Tractable OWL (TrOWL) Quill

Racer is the first OWL DL reasoner developed, and HermiT is the first publicly available OWL DL reasoner. Pellet is the most famous OWL DL reasoner. Protégé—the most widely used ontology development software—provides service for three OWL DL reasoners: Pellet, HermiT, and FaCT++. Pellet and HermiT support SWRL in DL-safe rules, meaning that rules will be applied only to known individuals. FaCT++ does not support rules at all. Pellet can work well with Jena API, while FaCT++ and HermiT cannot.

Rule engines include the following:

- **Cwm** is a simple forward-chaining reasoner developed in Python, which supports Notation3 (N3), RDF/XML, and N-Triples, with N3 being the major one. The results of rule evaluation are implementation dependent, as the semantics of N3 is not defined formally.

- **Euler** is a backward-chaining rule engine developed in Java and C# that also supports N3 notation.

- **Prolog:** The central concept in Prolog is backward chaining from a query. Prolog is really meant to be used from a console, even for end users; it is just about answering queries. Prolog is optimized, in a sense, for space—at the cost of speed. Examples of Prolog rules are the following:

father(A,B):- parent(A,B), Male (A).
hasUncle(X,Y):- hasParent(X,Z), hasBrother(Z,Y).

Common Logic: Common Logic is a collaboration on the Knowledge Interchange Format (KIF) and Concept Graph (CG). Its current version is Common Logic Interchange Format (CLIF). Syntax ((→ (and (parent?a?b) (male?a)) (father?a?b))).

Jess: The Java Expert System Shell (Jess) came along when Java was very young. Jess is a fully developed Java API inspired by CLIPS for building rule-based expert systems. It uses an improved form of the Rete (Latin for "net") algorithm to match patterns, i.e., facts in the knowledge base, to rules in the rule base. Jess has a Lisp-like syntax and is quite easy to learn and use. The rules can be written in two formats, XML or the Jess rule language, with the latter preferred. The central concept in Jess is forward chaining. Only developers type on a console; the command line is not intended for end users. Jess is about acting in response to inputs, not only answering queries. It uses forward chaining and the Rete algorithm, so the working memory must be populated with all relevant facts before execution of rules; this is not the case with SWRL, because of backward chaining. An example of Jess rule follows:

(def rule R1 (parent?a?b) (male?a) → (assert (father?a?b))).

2.7.6 Ontology Visualization

Most visualization tools available depict only certain aspects of an ontology. A very small number of visualization tools depict the complete ontologies. OWLViz, OntoTrack, and KC-Viz present a hierarchical layout showing only the class hierarchy of an ontology. Though OWLPropViz, OntoGraf, and FlexViz present the property relations along with the hierarchical layout, they do not show property characteristics. TGViz, NavigOWL, GrOWL, SOVA, RelFinder, and VOWL are some graph visualization tools; VOWL allows a user to explore complete ontologies and then zoom in to further explore the parts that require in-depth investigation.

References

Abaalkhail, Rana, Benjamin Guthier, Rajwa Alharthi, and Abdulmotaleb El Saddik. "Survey on ontologies for affective states and their influences." *Semantic Web* 9, no. 4 (2018): 441–458.

Ait-Ameur, Yamine, Mickaël Baron, Ladjel Bellatreche, Stéphane Jean, and Eric Sardet. "Ontologies in engineering: the OntoDB/OntoQL platform." *Soft Computing* 21, no. 2 (2017): 369–389.

Angele, Kevin, Dieter Fensel, Elwin Huaman, Elias Kärle, Oleksandra Panasiuk, Umutcan Şimşek, Ioan Toma, et al. "Semantic web empowered e-Tourism." In *Handbook of e-Tourism*, pp. 1–46. Springer, Cham, Switzerland, 2020.

Banane, Mouad, and Abdessamad Belangour. "A comparative study of RDF triple stores." Available at SSRN 3349399 (2019).

Berners-Lee, Tim, and James Hendler. "Publishing on the semantic web." *Nature* 410, no. 6832 (2001): 1023–1024.

Berners-Lee, Tim, James Hendler, and Ora Lassila. "The semantic web." *Scientific American* 284, no. 5 (2001): 34–43.

Chihoub, Houssem, Cédrine Madera, Christoph Quix, and Rihan Hai. "Architecture of data lakes." In *Databases and Big Data Set, Vol. 2: Data Lakes*, pp. 21–39. John Wiley & Sons, Hoboken, NJ, 2020.

Dentler, Kathrin, Ronald Cornet, Annette ten Teije, and Nicolette de Keizer. "Comparison of reasoners for large ontologies in the OWL 2 EL profile." *Semantic Web* 2, no. 2 (2011): 71–87.

Diène, Bassirou, Joel J. P. C. Rodrigues, Ousmane Diallo, El Hadji Malick Ndoye, and Valery V. Korotaev. "Data management techniques for Internet of Things." *Mechanical Systems and Signal Processing* 138 (2020): 106564.

Dorion, Eric, Christopher J. Matheus, and Mieczyslaw M. Kokar. "Towards a formal ontology for military coalitions operations." In *10th International Command & Control Research and Technology Symposium*, article 239. Department of Defense Command and Control Research Program, Washington, DC.

Ekren, Gülay, and Alptekin Erkollar. "The potential and capabilities of NoSQL databases for ERP systems." In *Advanced MIS and Digital Transformation for Increased Creativity and Innovation in Business*, pp. 147–168. IGI Global, Hershey, PA, 2020.

ElDahshan, K., E. K. Elsayed, and H. Mancy. "Semantic smart world framework." *Applied Computational Intelligence and Soft Computing* 2020 (2020): 8081578.

Euzenat, Jérôme, and Marie-Christine Rousset. "Semantic web." In *A Guided Tour of Artificial Intelligence Research, Vol. 3: Interfaces and Applications of Artificial Intelligence*, pp. 181–207. Springer, Cham, Switzerland, 2020.

Galgonek, Jakub, Tomáš Hurt, Vendula Michlíková, Petr Onderka, Jan Schwarz, and Jiří Vondrášek. "Advanced SPARQL querying in small molecule databases." *Journal of Cheminformatics* 8, no. 1 (2016): 31.

Haarslev, Volker, Kay Hidde, Ralf Möller, and Michael Wessel. "The RacerPro knowledge representation and reasoning system." *Semantic Web* 3, no. 3 (2012): 267–277.

Hewahi, Nabil M. Concept based censor production rules. International Journal of Decision Support System Technology (IJDSST), 10, no. 1 (2018): pp. 59–67.

Hooi, Yew Kwang, Fadzil Hassan, M., and Azmi Shariff, M., Ontology evaluation—A criteria selection framework. In 2015 International Symposium on Mathematical Sciences and Computing Research (iSMSC), pp. 298–303. IEEE, May 2015.

Jain, Sarika, and Sanju Mishra. "Knowledge representation with ontology." In *IJCA Proceedings on Advances in Computer Engineering and Applications*, ICACEA 6, pp. 1–5, 2014.

Jain, Sarika, Chhavi Gupta, and Amit Bhardwaj. "Research directions under the parasol of ontology based semantic web structure." In *Proceedings of the Eighth International Conference on Soft Computing and Pattern Recognition (SoCPaR 2016)*, pp. 644–655. Springer, Cham, Switzerland, 2016.

Kumar, Dikshit, Agam Kumar, Man Singh, Archana Patel, and Sarika Jain. "An online dictionary and thesaurus." *Journal of Artificial Intelligence Research & Advances* 6, no. 1 (2019): 32–38.

Malik, Sonika, and Sarika Jain. "Sup_Ont: an upper ontology." *International Journal of Web-Based Learning and Teaching Technologies* Unpublished 2020 .

Malik, Sonika, Sanju Mishra, N. K. Jain, and Sarika Jain. "Devising a super ontology." *Procedia Computer Science* 70 (2015): 785–792.

Mallik, Anupama, Hiranmay Ghosh, Santanu Chaudhury, and Gaurav Harit. "MOWL: an ontology representation language for web-based multimedia applications." *ACM Transactions on Multimedia Computing, Communications, and Applications* 10, no. 1 (2013): 8.

Mehla Sonia and Jain Sarika. "Rule languages for the semantic web." In Abraham A., Dutta P., Mandal J., Bhattacharya A., Dutta S. (eds) *Emerging Technologies in Data Mining and Information Security. Advances in Intelligent Systems and Computing*, Vol. 755. Springer, Singapore, 2019. https://doi.org/10.1007/978-981-13-1951-8_73.

Mishra, Sanju, and Sarika Jain. "A unified approach for OWL ontologies." *International Journal of Computer Science and Information Security* 14, no. 11 (2016): 747–754.

Mishra, Sanju, Sonika Malik, N. K. Jain, and Sarika Jain. "A realist framework for ontologies and the semantic web." *Procedia Computer Science* 70 (2015): 483–490.

Mishra, Sanju, Sarika Jain, Chhiteesh Rai, and Niketa Gandhi. "Security challenges in Semantic Web of Things." In *Innovations in Bio-Inspired Computing and Applications—IBICA 2018*, pp. 162–169. Springer, Cham, Switzerland, 2019.

Özsu, M. Tamer, and Patrick Valduriez. "NoSQL, NewSQL, and polystores." In *Principles of Distributed Database Systems*, pp. 519–557. Springer, Cham, Switzerland, 2020.

Patel, Archana, and Sarika Jain. "Formalisms of representing knowledge." *Procedia Computer Science* 125 (2018): 542–549.

Pellegrini, Tassilo, Victor Mireles, Simon Steyskal, Oleksandra Panasiuk, Anna Fensel, and Sabrina Kirrane. "Automated rights clearance using semantic web technologies: the DALICC framework." In *Semantic Applications*, pp. 203–218. Springer, Berlin, Germany, 2018.

Ra, Minyoung, Donghee Yoo, and Sungchun No. "Construction and applicability of military ontology for semantic data processing." In *Proceedings of the 3rd International Conference on Web Intelligence, Mining and Semantics*, article 15. Association for Computing Machinery, New York, NY, 2013.

Rashid, Pshtiwan Qader. *Semantic network and frame knowledge representation formalisms in artificial intelligence.* M. S. thesis, Eastern Mediterranean University (EMU), Famagusta, North Cyprus, 2015.

Rattanasawad Thanyalak, Kanda Runapongsa Saikaew,MarutBuranarach, and ThepchaiSupnithi. A review and comparison of rule languages and rule-based inference engines for the Semantic Web. In *2013 International Computer Science and Engineering Conference (ICSEC)*, pp. 1–6. IEEE, 2013. https://www.w3.org/Submission/SWRL/2013.

Shadbolt, Nigel, Tim Berners-Lee, and Wendy Hall. "The semantic web revisited." *IEEE Intelligent Systems* 21, no. 3 (2006): 96–101.

Smith, Barry, Kristo Miettinen, and William Mandrick. "The ontology of command and control (C2)." In *14th International Command & Control Research and Technology Symposium*, article 159. Department of Defense Command and Control Research Program, Washington, DC, 2009.

Tutcher, Jonathan. *Development of Semantic Data Models to Support Data Interoperability in the Rail Industry.* PhD diss., University of Birmingham, Birmingham, UK, 2016.

Tutcher, Jonathan, John M. Easton, and Clive Roberts. "Enabling data integration in the rail industry using RDF and OWL: the RaCoOn ontology." *ASCE-ASME Journal of Risk and Uncertainty in Engineering Systems, Part A: Civil Engineering* 3, no. 2 (2017): 859.

Uschold, Mike, and Michael Gruninger. "Ontologies: principles, methods and applications." *The Knowledge Engineering Review* 11, no. 2 (1996): 93–136.

Ye, Juan, Stamatia Dasiopoulou, Graeme Stevenson, Georgios Meditskos, Efstratios Kontopoulos, Ioannis Kompatsiaris, and Simon Dobson. "Semantic web technologies in pervasive computing: a survey and research roadmap." *Pervasive and Mobile Computing* 23 (2015): 1–25.

Yew, Kwang Hooi, M. Fadzil Hassan, and Azmi M. Shariff. "Ontology evaluation—a criteria selection framework." In *2015 International Symposium on Mathematical Sciences and Computing Research (iSMSC)*, pp. 298–303. IEEE 2015.

3

Semantics-Based Decision Support for Unconventional Emergencies

---

Efficient situation awareness and advice can be a boon to victims of emergencies. If decision makers are better aware of the situation they are in and similar situations that experts have handled in the past, and they are provided with advice, they will be in a better position to make prompt and meaningful decisions. Unconventional emergencies like earthquakes and terrorism are large-scale, sudden-onset, and repeating in nature, and thus create massive pressure on authorities and government agencies. The impact of such a calamity is global and transcends beyond social, economic, political, or geographic borders. A paradigm shift is required, with a holistic approach encompassing all facets of disaster management. The challenge is to strive toward preparedness backed by the coordination of all stakeholders. Efficient situation awareness is hampered by the temporal and spatial locality of human communications. Semantics-based decision support suggests utilizing semantic technologies during unconventional emergencies to spread situation awareness and provide advisory support.

3.1 The Problem

The International Emergency Management Society the Unites States Geological Survey, the World Bank, the Utah Geological Survey, and various agencies working under the United Nations System—such as the Food and Agriculture Organization (FAO), the International Labour Organization (ILO), UNICEF, UNESCO, United Nations University (UNU), United Nations Volunteers (UNV), the World Health Organization (WHO), and the World Meteorological Organization (WMO)—are contributing their part toward disaster risk reduction in order to address the underlying hazards and account for them systematically. Scientists and researchers have been working on potential impact scenarios, but the uncertainties and variability associated with disaster situations make traditional approaches inappropriate. The direct involvement of the public and the specific interests of victims and the government make the task even more challenging.

Currently various alert apps are in use to inform the public about any upcoming or ongoing disasters, any possible consequences of these disasters, instructions on how to behave in such situations, and protective measures to take [Dugdale et al. 2012, Avvenuti et al. 2014, Geldermann et al. 2009, Ngai et al. 2012, Vescoukis et al. 2012, Yu and Lai 2011, Hadiguna et al. 2014]. In unconventional emergencies, the major problem to be addressed is becoming aware of the situation you are in, then acting meticulously. Today, after more than 40 years of evolution, decision support systems have improved to intelligent systems capable of being utilized in many applications and all domains. Emergency management agencies, with the aid of intelligent decision support systems, have the responsibility of collaboratively contributing to reduce the aftermath of emergencies. They bring together national and international humanitarian services and resources in a timely and optimized manner.

A massive store of information is available about past disasters, in multiple forms and formats. The unorganized and inaccessible nature of this data makes it troublesome for policy and decision makers to do any analysis and respond in a timely manner. If this huge data is put in stores in a machine-understandable manner with distributed access, then algorithms can be written to assess the current situation and provide advisory support to decision makers. Practically, very little attention and effort has been spent in this direction. It has been observed, though, that post-disaster recovery is fueled by rapid and automated solutions to decision support, as experts are a scare resource and may be unavailable at the sudden outbreak of a disaster.

3.2 The Solution

In the terms of unconventional emergencies, situation awareness refers to the process of establishing a dynamic mechanism to analyze, predict, and judge the current situation and corresponding events in real time. The creation of a digital database and procedures will facilitate disaster risk reduction, damage assessment, and monitoring of major natural hazards. There is a need to develop appropriate techniques and tools for decision support not only to recommend actions but to place in front of decision makers a menu of options to choose from [Chen et al. 2013, Rahaman and Hossain 2013, Sahebjamnia et al. 2017].

This book presents to the prototypical development of a knowledge-driven situation awareness and advisory support (KDSAAS) which provides real-time information in order to provide intelligent decision support. The goal of KDSAAS is to address the short-term direct effects of an emergency incident to limit injuries, loss of life, damage to property, and any unfavorable outcomes by

- planning for and managing the consequences of emergency incidents using available resources in the critical hours.
- providing details of past incidents along with awareness for incoming emergencies.
- supporting end users in making the best decisions by providing enhanced and real-time situation awareness.

For this book, a case study of emergency situations has been chosen for demonstration purposes. The aim of this case study is to familiarize readers with the usage of various approaches and tools to provide situation awareness and advisory support to end users in a seamless manner. With such a system in place, the rescue team and society will be better informed, and decision makers will find themselves in a better situation to counter the disaster and restore a safe state. Technologies standardized by the World Wide Web Consortium (W3C) have been utilized for representing, storing, querying, evaluating, and further enriching knowledge.

As advocated in Chapter 1, semantic intelligence can be achieved by storing semantically rich data, represented as a semantic data model, in semantic repositories that are self-optimizing and explainable for enterprise-wide knowledge collaboration. There exist multiple illustrations in the literature of using ontologies to represent the domain knowledge of disasters [Bouyerbou et al. 2019, Kontopoulos et al. 2018, Jain et al. 2016, Lama and Jain 2019, Xu et al. 2014, Bitencourt et al. 2015, Yu et al. 2008, Joshi et al. 2007, Fan and Zlatanova 2011, Mishra and Jain 2019]. The complete knowledge treasure/knowledge repository/knowledge store (data and processes) of KDSAAS is depicted here:

Knowledge Store/Treasure/ Repository = Procedural Knowledge + Declarative Knowledge
Declarative Knowledge = Domain Ontology + Domain Case Base + Domain Rule Base
Domain Ontology = Domain Schema (TBOX) + Domain data (ABOX)

The presence of such a centralized knowledge store facilitates researchers and decision makers in

- training rescue teams
- assessing risks
- interacting with competent authorities
- joint planning
- better understanding of linkages and undertaking a range of analyses

The centralized knowledge stores comprise declarative knowledge (what) and procedural knowledge (how). Explicit knowledge—like the domain ontologies, domain case bases of history cases, and domain rule bases of domain expert knowledge—is declarative knowledge. All the common procedures, like a resource manager or a recommendation engine, constitute procedural knowledge. The domain ontology organizes and stores the emergency data as Resource Description Framework (RDF) statements which are further of two types, TBox or ABox. TBox statements are those involving concepts and are also called the domain schema. ABox statements are those involving instances and are also called the domain data. An example of a TBox statement is "all terrorist attacks are emergencies"; an example of an ABox statement is "Al-Qaeda is a terrorist organization." The goal of the system constitutes following work elements (tasks). Figure 3.1 presents the system architecture of KDSAAS.

1. **Knowledge Representation and Storage:** This involves the development of the declarative knowledge to be utilized. For KDSAAS, two sample domain ontologies have been created—the earthquake ontology (EO) and the terrorism ontology (TO)—along with the corresponding case bases and rule bases to test the various use cases.

   a. **Developing Domain Ontologies:** Domain ontologies are constructed using existing state-of-the-art methodologies. The test cases have been created for two types of emergency—earthquake and terrorism—so two domain ontologies, namely the EO and the TO have been created.

   b. Archiving Past Experiences (Storing Cases)

   c. Acquiring Expertise (Codifying Rules)

2. **Resource Manager:** KDSAAS also provides an intelligent resource manager as a model for situation awareness, providing better interoperability of heterogeneous resources for emergency-situation information. The resource manager provides the end-users of KDSAAS a real-time holistic situation overview and resource-management assistance. This increased situation awareness improves the capacity to comprehend and tackle the problem at hand within a time constraint. The procedures for the resource manager utilize the domain ontologies to interact with the user.

3. **Advisory System:** There are multiple illustrations in the literature of the use of ontologies to recommend appropriate actions in the domain of disasters [Anbarasi and Mayilvahanan 2017, Zhong et al. 2016, Jain et al. 2019, Kou et al. 2014, Luo et al. 2016, De Maio et al. 2011, Zhang et al. 2016, Malizia et al. 2009, Onorati et al. 2014, Han and Xu 2015, Roeloffs and Goltz 2017]. KDSAAS demonstrates

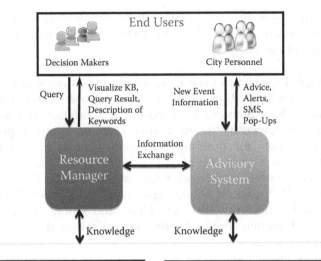

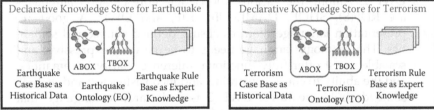

FIGURE 3.1
System Architecture of KDSAAS

an ontology-supported hybrid reasoning framework for generating advice by utilizing best practices, i.e., decision trees, ontological representation, case-based reasoning, and rule-based reasoning (RBR). This framework generates recommendations with proper justification based on past experiences and experts' codified knowledge. The advisory system provides KDSAAS the ability to learn from past emergency situations and generate recommendations with proper justification for new problems based on past solutions and experts' knowledge. It utilizes all three components—i.e., the domain knowledge base (ontology), the domain case base, and the domain rule base–to provide advice.

3.3 Tools and Techniques

To achieve the goals of KDSAAS, different tools, techniques, platforms, languages, and integrated development environments have been utilized.

Chapter 2 discusses the various alternatives available. This section presents and summarizes the tools utilized for KDSAAS, all of which are primarily open source in nature.

1. **Protégé:** Protégé has been used for general-purpose environments and as ontology editor tool. It is a free, extensible, and open-source framework by Stanford University that is extensively used by the corporate, government, and academic communities. It provides a suite of tools for building intelligent systems with ontologies. Protégé has a plug-and-play architecture with plug-ins to allow back-end/interface extensions, like an OWL plugin (Protégé-OWL) to edit OWL and RDF ontologies and SWRL rules. Protégé has a visual editor for OWL (OWLViz) and storage back ends for Jena and Sesame. Today, Protégé is available in desktop and web versions.

2. **OWL 2:** Among the various knowledge-representation languages are RDF(S), SHOE, DAML+OIL, KIF, and OWL. A good representation language requires clearly defined syntax and semantics. The ontology language needs to be natural, expressive, and scalable; must offer fully functional inference, clarity in semantics, and the ability to check constraints and inconsistencies; and include some desirable features. OWL 2 is a declarative language that performs reasoning with large numbers of instances and provides a great deal of expressivity and conciseness to represent the knowledge model. It has been chosen as the knowledge-representation language to create the ontology of resources and emergency information.

3. **SPARQL:** SPARQL Protocol and RDF Query Language (pronounced "sparkle") has been used to express queries. It is a W3C recommendation and has become a standard semantic query language for querying across data sources (any data source that is in RDF or can be mapped to RDF triple stores). There exist tools to translate other query languages, like SQL and XQuery, to SPARQL and vice versa. There also exist tools to convert a natural language into SPARQL for querying an RDF store.

4. **Java:** The choice of programming language is mostly a matter of comfort. The Java programming language has powerful libraries and an Apache Jena framework for working with RDF and OWL ontologies, so that the reasoning capabilities of OWL can be used in Java applications. Documentation and community support for Java is also readily available. Java is a dominant high-level imperative programming language and has been used to develop all the procedures of parsing the emergency information into usable format, situation awareness, and decision support.

5. **NetBeans:** The application developed is Java based, so the NetBeans integrated development environment platform has been used, and all the user interfaces built in it. It supports the Jena framework as well as the OWL API.

6. **Jena API:** Jena API has been utilized as the programming tool kit because it is one of the most popular APIs for manipulating ontologies in Java. Jena facilitates storing RDF triples and allows manipulation (addition, removal, querying, inference) of the information in these triples. In KDSAAS, Jena is utilized by writing Java programs, as opposed to command-line tools. It is fundamentally an RDF platform, so it is suitable for (and only for) ontologies like RDFS and OWL ontologies which are built over RDF. Ontologies can be read and inferenced like with any other ontology reasoner.

7. **Jena Generic Rule Reasoner:** SWRL results are treated as asserted statements, which would not be very practical in this system, as whenever the RBR module is consulted, the results will be asserted to the ontology, affecting future requests. The Jena rules have been stored in text files. Whenever a change or update is required in the rules, it can be done by just editing the text file. The Jena generic reasoner performs RBR on the rule base (Jena rules) and provides recommendations.

8. **Pellet:** During the developed ontology's evaluation, its consistency and correctness must be checked. The Pellet DL reasoner has been utilized for inferring implicit knowledge and checking the consistency of the ontology. Pellet is an open-source Java-based OWL DL reasoner with a number of unique features. It is a product from Clark and Parsia, a small research and development firm in Washington, DC. Pellet can support almost all the species of OWL 1 and OWL 2, and it can be downloaded and embedded in other applications. It supports and hence can be used in conjunction with both Jena and OWL API libraries.

9. **VOWL:** VOWL, i.e., Visual Notation for OWL Ontologies, has been utilized as a comprehensive visual language for visualizing the developed ontologies. The ontologies need to be converted into the corresponding JSON files.

References

Anbarasi, C., and P. Mayilvahanan. "Humanitarian assistance ontology implementation during disaster management in Chennai flood-2015 using text mining techniques." *International Journal of Pure and Applied Mathematics* 116, no. 21 (2017): 729–739.

Avvenuti, Marco, Stefano Cresci, Andrea Marchetti, Carlo Meletti, and Maurizio Tesconi. "EARS (earthquake alert and report system): a real time decision support system for earthquake crisis management." In *Proceedings of the 20th ACM SIGKDD International Conference on Knowledge Discovery and Data Mining*, pp. 1749–1758. Association for Computing Machinery, New York, NY, 2014.

Bitencourt, Kattiuscia, Frederico Durão, and Manoel Mendonça. "EmergencyFire: an ontology for fire emergency situations." In *Proceedings of the 21st Brazilian Symposium on Multimedia and the Web*, pp. 73–76. Association for Computing Machinery, New York, NY, 2015.

Bouyerbou, Hafidha, Kamal Bechkoum, and Richard Lepage. "Geographic ontology for major disasters: methodology and implementation." *International Journal of Disaster Risk Reduction* 34 (2019): 232–242.

Chen, Shyi-Ming, Yun-Hou Huang, and Rung-Ching Chen. "A recommendation system for anti-diabetic drugs selection based on fuzzy reasoning and ontology techniques." *International Journal of Pattern Recognition and Artificial Intelligence* 27, no. 04 (2013): 1359001.

De Maio, Carmen, Giuseppe Fenza, Matteo Gaeta, Vincenzo Loia, and Francesco Orciuoli. "A knowledge-based framework for emergency DSS." *Knowledge-Based Systems* 24, no. 8 (2011): 1372–1379.

Dugdale, Julie, Bartel Van de Walle, and Corinna Koeppinghoff. "Social media and SMS in the Haiti earthquake." In *Proceedings of the 21st International Conference on World Wide Web*, pp. 713–714. Association for Computing Machinery, New York, NY, 2012.

Fan, Zhengjie, and Sisi Zlatanova. "Exploring ontologies for semantic interoperability of data in emergency response." *Applied Geomatics* 3, no. 2 (2011): 109–122.

Geldermann, Jutta, Valentin Bertsch, Martin Treitz, Simon French, Konstantinia N. Papamichail, and Raimo P. Hämäläinen. "Multi-criteria decision support and evaluation of strategies for nuclear remediation management." *Omega* 37, no. 1 (2009): 238–251.

Hadiguna, Rika Ampuh, Insannul Kamil, Azalika Delati, and Richard Reed. "Implementing a web-based decision support system for disaster logistics: a case study of an evacuation location assessment for Indonesia." *International Journal of Disaster Risk Reduction* 9 (2014): 38–47.

Han, Yaoci, and Wei Xu. "An ontology-oriented decision support system for emergency management based on information fusion." In *Proceedings of the 1st ACM SIGSPATIAL International Workshop on the Use of GIS in Emergency Management*, pp. 1–8. Association for Computing Machinery, New York, NY, 2015.

Jain, Sarika, Sonia Mehla, and Sanju Mishra. "An ontology of natural disasters with exceptions." In *2016 International Conference System Modeling & Advancement in Research Trends (SMART)*, pp. 232–237. IEEE, 2016.

Jain, Sarika, Sonia Mehla, and Apoorv Gaurav Agarwal. "An ontology based earthquake recommendation system." In *Advanced Informatics for Computing Research—ICAICR 2018*, pp. 331–340. Springer, Singapore, 2019.

Joshi, Hemant, Remzi Seker, Coskun Bayrak, Srini Ramaswamy, and Jeffrey B. Connelly. "Ontology for disaster mitigation and planning." In *Proceedings of the 2007 Summer Computer Simulation Conference*, article 26. Society for Computer Simulation International, pp. 1–18, San Diego, CA, 2007.

Kontopoulos, Efstratios, Panagiotis Mitzias, Jürgen Moßgraber, Philipp Hertweck, Hylke van der Schaaf, Désiré Hilbring, Francesca Lombardo, et al. "Ontology-based representation of crisis management procedures for climate events." In *Proceedings of the 15th ISCRAM Conference*, pp. 1064–1073. Rochester Institute of Technology, Rochester, NY, 2018.

Kou, Gang, Daji Ergu, and Yu Shi. "An integrated expert system for fast disaster assessment." *Computers & Operations Research* 42 (2014): 95–107.

Lama, Vishal, and Sarika Jain. "Digitization of disaster management: a multimedia ontological approach." In *Information and Communication Technology for Competitive Strategies*, pp. 197–203. Springer, Singapore, 2019.

Luo, Hanbin, Xiaofan Peng, and Botao Zhong. "Application of ontology in emergency plan management of metro operation." *Procedia Engineering* 164 (2016): 158–165.

Malizia, Alessio, Pablo Acuña, Teresa Onorati, Paloma Diaz, and Ignacio Aedo. "CAP-ONES: an emergency notification system for all." *International Journal of Emergency Management* 6, no. 3–4 (2009): 302–316.

Mishra, Sanju, and Sarika Jain. "Towards a semantic knowledge treasure for military intelligence." In *Emerging Technologies in Data Mining and Information Security*, pp. 835–845. Springer, Singapore, 2019.

Ngai, E. W. T., T. K. P. Leung, Y. H. Wong, M. C. M. Lee, P. Y. F. Chai, and Y. S. Choi. "Design and development of a context-aware decision support system for real-time accident handling in logistics." *Decision Support Systems* 52, no. 4 (2012): 816–827.

Onorati, Teresa, Alessio Malizia, Paloma Diaz, and Ignacio Aedo. "Modeling an ontology on accessible evacuation routes for emergencies." *Expert Systems with Applications* 41, no. 16 (2014): 7124–7134.

Roeloffs, Evelyn, and James Goltz. "The California earthquake advisory plan: a history." *Seismological Research Letters* 88, no. 3 (2017): 784–797.

Bouyerbou, Hafidha, Kamal Bechkoum, and Richard Lepage. "Geographic ontology for major disasters: Methodology and implementation" *International journal of disaster risk reduction* 34 (2019): 232–242.

Vescoukis, Vassilios, Nikolaos Doulamis, and Sofia Karagiorgou. "A service oriented architecture for decision support systems in environmental crisis management." *Future Generation Computer Systems* 28, no. 3 (2012): 593–604.

Xu, Jinghai, Timothy L. Nyerges, and Gaozhong Nie. "Modeling and representation for earthquake emergency response knowledge: perspective for working with geo-ontology." *International Journal of Geographical Information Science* 28, no. 1 (2014): 185–205.

Yu, Kai, Qingquan Wang, and Lili Rong. "Emergency ontology construction in emergency decision support system." In *2008 IEEE International Conference on Service Operations and Logistics, and Informatics, Vol. 1*, pp. 801–805. IEEE, 2008.

Yu, Lean, and Kin Keung Lai. "A distance-based group decision-making methodology for multi-person multi-criteria emergency decision support." *Decision Support Systems* 51, no. 2 (2011): 307–315.

Zhang, Fushen, Shaobo Zhong, Simin Yao, Chaolin Wang, and Quanyi Huang. "Ontology-based representation of meteorological disaster system and its application in emergency management: illustration with a simulation case study of comprehensive risk assessment." *Kybernetes* 45, no. 5 (2016): 798–814.

Zhong, Shao-bo, Chao-lin Wang, Guan-nan yao, and Quan-yi Huang. "Emergency decision of meteorological disasters: a geo-ontology based perspective." In *2016 International Conference on Computational Modeling, Simulation and Applied Mathematics (CMSAM 2016)*. DEStech Publications, Lancaster, PA, 2016.

4

Knowledge Representation and Storage

Emergency information sharing between government entities and policy and decision makers is possible by the presence of centralized disaster knowledge stores. The knowledge stored in this store should be represented in a format that allows easy exchange of information between different parties involved. If the knowledge is exchangeable in real time, the speed and quality of the coordinated response increases. In order to free up data from storage in isolated silos and to enable machines to understand and interpret the meaning of information, we must set up a network of links between structured data. Semantic data models and semantic repositories are a solution for this. This chapter explains the process of creating knowledge stores for two disasters under study, namely earthquake and terrorism. Each domain-specific centralized knowledge store comprises a domain ontology, a case base of history cases, a rule base of expert knowledge, and required common procedures according to the use case scenario.

4.1 Developing Knowledge Stores

Making quick decisions according to available resources during an emergency is a very challenging endeavor. Emergency data is available in databases, knowledge bases, text documents, and video and audio. Text documents, video, and audio do not provide inference over the data. In predicting emergencies and generating alerts and recommendations afterward, emergency data from different sources is to be integrated and made interoperable for specific, certain, accurate, and precise access. The codification of the meanings of terms completes the system of knowledge representation and storage.

This chapter incorporates developing declarative knowledge stores of the two domains under consideration, namely the earthquake knowledge store (EKS) and terrorism knowledge store (TKS). Each knowledge store comprises the complete knowledge of that domain (ontology, case base, and rule base) required by the common procedures for providing situation awareness and generating advice. Ontologies describe the meaning (i.e., the semantics) of content in a way that can be interpreted by machines. Past experiences of emergencies are stored as cases in the case base, and expert knowledge is codified in the form of rules in the rule base.

4.2 Developing Ontologies

With the dramatic increase in data worldwide, it is no longer possible to extract value from it without making semantics explicit. Real-world problems use real-time systems that are resource constrained; they should work very effectively and accurately within the given resources for the system response. The heterogeneity of data produces variation in meaning or ambiguity in the interpretation of entity; as a result, it prevents information sharing between systems. Therefore, without identification of the semantic mappings between entities we cannot communicate, interact, collaborate, or share information across applications. Available representation schemes and their specific flavors vary in level of power and expressivity. An ontology is prominently used for representing knowledge because of its expressive power [Staab et al. 2001, Welty and Guarino 2001]. Knowledge, when represented in the form of an ontology, procures an intelligent response to a query posed by a user. An ontology is developed use in applications which need to process or transfer the contents of information instead of only displaying information to an agent. An ontology provides greater machine interpretability and interoperability of content by defining the relationship between vocabularies along with formal semantics.

4.2.1 Defining Ontology

Databases for emergency response exist that provide real-time and graphical information to responders. But a major issue in such databases is interoperability. All these databases are in different formats, and they are not able to communicate with each other or exchange information. In addition, traditional relational databases store data in tabular form, without any focus on its inherent meaning.

Knowledge-representation formalisms are used to represent machine-understandable semantics. They provide efficient information storage and retrieval along with reasoning power. Various knowledge-representation formalisms have been spawned, each having its own set of features and trade-offs. These formalisms differ from each other in the way that knowledge is compiled, the extent of the descriptions offered, and the type of inference power sanctioned. Some of the better-known formalisms for knowledge representation are semantic networks, frame systems, rules, and logic; the logic-based knowledge-representation formalism called an ontology is widely used.

A genuine effort is going on across the globe, among researchers at different institutions and industry people from different fields and disciplines, to shift all their data to a semantic format. The usage of semantic technologies is going to be a paradigm shift. Many researchers in academia and developers in industry are already onboard to use semantic technologies in medicine, aeronautics, social networks, e-commerce, and many more areas. The biggest users include Facebook, Wikipedia (DBpedia, Wikidata), the BBC, Volkswagen UK, and Google. With proper and intelligent usage of semantic technologies, information will be represented in a structured form and searched for, retrieved, and processed automatically by machines. The machines will then be able to reason and yield much information that is not even stated explicitly. Semantic technologies even facilitate the automated consumption of such produced information.

Semantic technologies solve such issues by virtue of adopting Uniform Resource Identifiers (URIs) and ontologies. URIs are the unique identifiers for all the domain items (concepts, attributes, things, events, relationships, or any other metadata), called resources. The purpose of these identifiers is to uniquely identify the domain terms and remove any ambiguities from information. Further, an ontology is the set of all items in the domain model. Ontologies represent the domain knowledge or the world around us in a manner that it is understandable by machines so that machines are able to reason over it. After knowledge is represented in the form of ontologies, machines will be able not only to understand and interpret information but also to deduce its accuracy and deduce new facts from already-existing ones. Ontologies allow both taxonomic and non-taxonomic relationships between the terms; both types of relationship make it possible for machines to infer new implicit information.

An ontology is a precise explanation of entities and reasoning in a domain under discussion. By using ontologies, a computer can act as if it has understood the information it is handling and is able to utilize it in reasoning. An ontology is a means of representing semantic knowledge and includes at least classes, properties, relations, instances, and axioms. Properties are of two types: data and object properties. Different authors have provided different tuples for defining an ontology to manifest real-world terms. Some of those tuples are depicted in Table 4.1. Kindly note that the attributes of tuple have been expanded only once on its first occurrence, unless its expansion is changed.

TABLE 4.1

Ontological Tuples

Reference	Ontology Tuple
Ehrig and Sure 2004	$(C, H_C, R_C, H_R, I, R_I, A)$ C: Concepts of the schema H_C: Subsumption hierarchy in which the concepts are arranged. R_C: Relations that exist between single concepts. H_R: Hierarchy of relations I: Instances of a specific concept R_I: Relations that exist between Instances. A: Axioms/Rules/Propositions that can be used to infer knowledge from already existing one.
Ehrig et al. 2005	$(C, H_C, R_C, H_R, I, R_I, \iota C, \iota R, A)$ ιC: instantiation connection between C and R_C ιR: instantiation connection between R_C and R_I
Niepert et al. 2008	$(C, H_C, H_R, L, F_C, F_R)$ $(C, H_C, H_R, L, F_C, F_R)$ H_R: Set of non-taxonomic relations L: set of terms (lexicals) which refer to concepts and relations F_C, F_R: relations that map the terms in L to the corresponding concepts and relations.
Zhang and Xia 2008	(C, R) C: set of representational terms called conceptions R: set of relationships among those conceptions.
Chen et al. 2010	(C, P, I, S) P: set of relationships/properties S: Axioms
Ngo et al. 2012	$(C, P, T, I, H_C, H_P, A)$ T: set of datatypes H_P: hierarchy of relationships
Salahi and Ansarinia 2013	(C, H^C, R, H^R, I) H^C: same as H_C R: set of relations between two classes H_R: Hierarchy of relations I: individuals of classes (C) or relations (R).
Yap and Kim 2013	(C, R, H^C, rel, A^0) rel: set of non-taxonomic relations A^0: same as A
Kalfoglou and Schorlemmer 2003	(S, A) S: the ontological signature — describing the vocabulary (i.e. the terms that lexicalize concepts and relations between concepts).
Kotis et al. 2006; Hooi et al. 2014	(S, A) This is a slight variation of the definition given in [Kalfoglou and Schorlemmer 2003], where S is also equipped with a partial order, based on the inclusion relation between concepts. In our definition, conforming to description logics'

(Continued)

TABLE 4.1
(Continued)

Reference	Ontology Tuple
	terminological axioms, inclusion relations are ontological axioms included in A.
Xue et al. 2014	(C, P, I)
Xue and Wang 2015; Xue and Pan 2018	$(C, P, I, A, \leq_C, \leq_P, \phi_{CP}, \phi_{CI}, \phi_{PI})$ $\leq_C$ is a partial order on C, called class hierarchy or taxonomy, $\leq_P$ is a partial order on P, called property hierarchy, $\phi_{CP}: P \rightarrow C \times C$ is a function which associates a property $p \in P$ with two linked classes through the property p. $\phi_{CI}: C \rightarrow P(I)$ is a function which associates a concept $c \in C$ with a subset of I representing the instances of the concept c, $\phi_{PI}: P \rightarrow P(I^2)$ is a function which associates a property $p \in P$ with a subset of Cartesian product $I \times I$ representing the pair of instances related through the property p.
Fellah et al., 2019	(C, R, H_C, I) $R \subseteq C \times C$ is the set of relations over concepts $H_C \subseteq R$ is a subset of R, represents hierarchical relation set between concepts
Adnan, M., & Afzal, M., 2017	(C, I, P, R_H, R_C) R_H: the class hierarchy R_C: the association among individual classes.
Ait-Ameur et al. 2017	(E, OC, A, SuperEntities, TypeOf, AttDomain, AttRange, Val) E is a set of entities representing the ontology language. It includes predefined entities such as the constructor of classes C and properties P as well as user-defined entities. OC is the set of ontology elements (classes, properties ...). They have a unique identifier. A is the set of attributes describing each ontology element. For example, classes are described with names which can be defined in different natural languages. SuperEntities:$E \rightarrow 2^E$ is a partial function which defines the super-entities of an entity. TypeOf:OC$\rightarrow$E defines the type of an ontology element. For example *Ball_Bearing* is an instance of the C entity. AttributeDomain, AttributeRange: A$\rightarrow$E define, respectively, the domain and range of each attribute. Val: OC$\times$A$\rightarrow$OC defines the value that an ontology element has for a given attribute.
Soui et al. 2017	(C, P, H_C, H_R, R) R: SWRL adaptation rules (Semantic Web Rule Language). (C, R, H_C, H_R, rel, I)

(Continued)

TABLE 4.1
(*Continued*)

Reference	Ontology Tuple
Ehrig and Staab 2004, Wan et al., 2018	
Qin et al., 2018	(S_C, S_P, S_I, S_A)
	S_C is a set of classes, S_P is a set of properties, S_I is a set of individuals, and S_A is a set of axioms
Staab and Studer 2010, Cheng et al., 2019	(C, R, A, I)
Euzenat and Shvaiko 2007, Mohammadi et al., 2019	(C, DP, OP, I)
	DP: set of data properties explaining the characteristics of the classes
	OP: set of object properties defining the relation of two classes;
Lamurias et al., 2019	(C, R)

Table 4.1 shows that every author has concentrated on an ontological tuple rather than focus on formalization of classes or concepts of the ontology that are the heart of the representation of real-world entities.

4.2.2 Methodology

Researchers have provided various methodologies for the design and construction of ontologies [An and Park 2018, Mishra and Jain 2014, Corcho et al. 2003, Paredes-Moreno et al. 2010, Farquhar et al. 1997]. All of these methodologies provide systematic guidelines toward rigorous construction of ontologies, but they revolve around five basic steps, which the development of the earthquake ontology and terrorism ontology also follow: scope determination, concept identification, concept analysis and organization, encoding, and evaluation.

4.2.2.1 Scope Determination

This phase determines the scope of the ontology by providing the answer to the question "Why are we going to develop it?" Table 4.2 shows sets of competence questions for the EO and TO that provide a better understanding of the scope. Their correct answers were determined by consulting subject matter experts.

For the EO, the following sources were utilized for data collection:

- Subject matter experts
- Existing terrorism portals
- Websites like Google and Wikipedia
- Interviews with many military commanders

TABLE 4.2

Competency Questions

Competency Questions for Earthquake Ontology (EO)	
1.	Name the relief items provided to persons affected by disaster X.
2.	List the actions taken during the Bhuj earthquake.
3.	Display all the different emergency situations, along with all their subtypes.
4.	What are some of the major causes of an earthquake?
5.	Which instruments are used to measure the intensity of natural disaster X?
6.	Display the flood-prone regions in a given area.

Competency Questions for Terrorism Ontology (TO)	
1.	Name the helicopters that are used only for attack.
2.	Display the total number of attacks per country through a given date.
3.	Which branch of the Indian Army handles the Army Aviation Corps?
4.	Display total casualties (deaths and injuries) by state.
5.	What is the number of casualties caused by terrorist organizations?
6.	List attacks by state, with complete descriptions.
7.	On which terrains do artillery regiments operate?
8.	Name the operation which handled the Pathankot attack.
9.	Display all operations that have been undertaken by Indian military forces.
10.	Display the names of regiments according to seniority level.
11.	What is the name of the workshop that was used in Operation Parakram?
12.	Display the name of the attack that caused the most casualties.

- Existing ontologies such as Munin
- Research articles and websites

For the TO, the following sources were used:

- Research papers from journals and conferences [Deaton et al. 2005, Ding et al. 2017, Knoke 2015, Houghton 2008, Gilbert 2018, Schuurman 2018]
- Existing terrorism portals, including the South Asia Terrorism Portal (https://www.satp.org) [Wilkerson et al. 2005]
- Web articles (Wikipedia, news sites, etc.)
- The Global Terrorism Database
- Interviews with military personnel, Indian forces, and the general public
- Annual Report 2017–18, Ministry of Home Affairs, Government of India
- 2018 Global Peace Index report
- *Patterns of Global Terrorism* 2017 [*Global Terrorism Index* 2017, LaFree 2010]
- The RAND Database of Worldwide Terrorism Incidents (https://www.rand.org/nsrd/projects/terrorism-incidents.html)

4.2.2.2 Concept Identification

This phase involves identifying the fundamental concepts and relationships, their attributes, instances, any constraints, and restrictions.

4.2.2.3 Concept Analysis and Organization

This step involves analyzing the terms and building the conceptual model by binding the terms into a hierarchy. All the terms are organized in a precise structure with taxonomic and non-taxonomic relationships. The terms identified as concepts or entities are arranged from the top down with increasing specificity in parent-child relationships. In this way, the ontology grows vertically as a TBox. The items identified as instances or individuals are attached to their corresponding concepts. In this way, the ontology grows horizontally as an ABox.

4.2.2.4 Encoding

This step involves transcribing the structure in some knowledge-description language. Various knowledge-description languages are available, including RDFS, OWL, and SKOS. OWL was utilized to develop both the EO and the TO.

4.2.2.5 Evaluation

This step involves testing the quality of captured data. To evaluate our ontologies, both external and internal evaluations have been undertaken. External evaluation was achieved by writing competency questions to inquire whether the knowledge stores were efficient enough to respond to them. During the internal evaluation, the Pellet reasoner was utilized as part of Protégé to verify consistency. The competency questions were written in SPARQL query language and executed on Pellet. Section 4.3 evaluates both the EO and TO.

4.2.3 SupOnt-EO

The EO and TO domain ontologies are integrated with the upper ontology SupOnt, which allows for modeling any environment [Malik and Jain in press]. It accommodates complete information of the entities and has the ability to integrate with the domain ontologies. SupOnt contains all the features that are required to represent the context. Figure 4.1 depicts the taxonomy of SupOnt-EO for earthquake situations, but any domain ontology can be similarly integrated. The upper part of the figure shows a few concepts of the SupOnt ontology, and lower part displays some of the concepts of the EO. SupOnt-EO illustrates three levels of knowledge: an

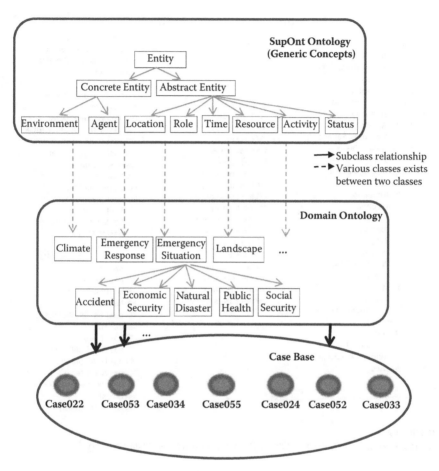

FIGURE 4.1
Taxonomy of SupOnt-EO for Earthquake Situations

upper-level ontology of generic concepts, the domain ontology of emergencies, and the individuals as the set of cases.

Figure 4.2 shows the classification of concepts along with object and data properties of the EO. The earthquake ontology represents information about emergency situations like natural disasters, accidental disasters, economic security, public health, social security, and the consequences of an emergency situation. Figure 4.3 shows the classification of concepts along with object and data properties of the TO. The terrorism ontology represents information about emergency situations like equipment, workshops, attacks, operations, armaments, location, building, hospital, and other information regarding military resources, along with all terrorist attacks which have happened. Figure 4.3 shows the hierarchal representation of the

(a)   (b)   (c)

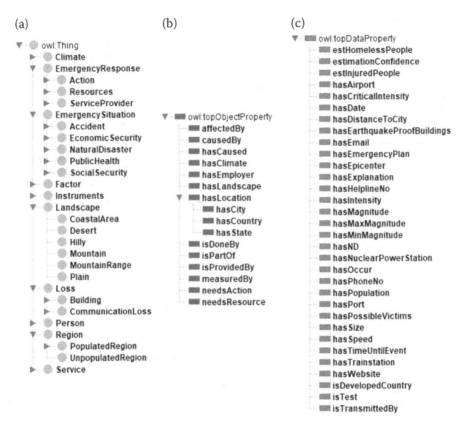

FIGURE 4.2
(a) Classification of EO, (b) Top Object Property, and (c) Top Data Property

classes of the TO with subclass and superclass relationships; for example, the class "Disaster" is a subclass of "Emergency" because it is placed below "Emergency" with an edge, and the class "Emergency" is a superclass of "Disaster" because it is placed above "Disaster" with an edge. The hierarchical representation of the TO is taken from Protégé.

4.3 Evaluation of Ontologies

There exists no standard approach for evaluation, as each ontology deals with a different domain, and some ambiguity is always involved [Guarino and Welty 2004, Keet et al. 2013, Poveda-Villalón et al. 2014, Bilgin et al. 2014].

(a)   (b)   (c)

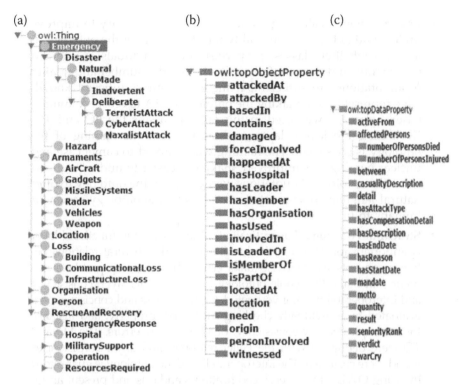

FIGURE 4.3
(a) Classification of TO, (b) Top Object Property, and (c) Top Data Property

The evaluation framework followed to evaluate the EO and TO is a combination of several pre-existing and reliable evaluation methods and tools. The evaluation was performed in two phases:

- Verification, which refers to building the ontology correctly
- Validation, which refers to building the correct ontology

This simplifies the evaluation by ensuring that each characteristic of the ontology is evaluated separately instead of evaluating the ontology as a whole [Jain and Meyer 2018].

4.3.1 Evaluation by Verification

In evaluation by verification, the encoding of the specification is checked, to make sure that the ontology confirms to the specified quality criteria. In the verification phase, evaluation is done in two layers: lexical and structural/functional.

- **Lexical Layer:** Evaluating the lexical layer is necessary to improve understandability and reusability for other users of the ontology. It assesses whether classes, properties, and individuals are named consistently and meaningfully and whether the number and quality of annotations are sufficient. It thereby ensures sufficient knowledge representation, making the ontology easier to reuse. A human-based approach was used in this layer to assess the EO and TO. Evaluating the lexical layer assesses whether the naming of the ontology is consistent. The naming was adapted to camel case and unclear naming was improved, making it easier to understand and reuse the ontology. Annotations were added in the ontology to offer natural language documentation and make the ontology easier for humans to understand.

- **Structural/Functional Layer:** Evaluating the structural/functional layer is important for assessing the hierarchical and structural relations between concepts, as otherwise major errors and reasoning problems can occur that make the whole ontology useless. In this layer, consistency and interoperability are investigated. Completeness and conciseness are evaluated by individually checking each class, property, and instance for incompleteness, inconsistency, or redundancy errors. The EO and TO were debugged with the Pellet reasoner, and any inconsistencies found were corrected. The interoperability of the ontology is guaranteed by using OWL 2 to preserve codification standards and present an interoperable knowledge platform. This layer can be evaluated via metric-based, criteria-based, and cost-based approaches.

4.3.1.1 Metric-Based Evaluation

Various tools, such as OntoMetrics, OntoClean, and OntoQA, are available for evaluating ontologies quantitatively. The EO and TO were evaluated with the OntoMetrics tool to calculate their statistics. Table 4.3 shows the values of the metrics for both ontologies, collectively showing how much knowledge is encoded in each ontology.

- **Base metric:** The base metric includes simple parameters such as class count (CC), axiom count (AC), object property count (OPC), data property count (DPC), and individual count (IC), among many more. The tools in Protégé and OntoMetrics were employed to measure these various parameters.

- **Schema metric:** The design of the ontology is evaluated by the schema metric. This metric addresses attribute richness (AR), inheritance richness (IR), relationship richness (RR), the axiom/class ratio (A/C R), the inverse relation ratio (IRR), and the class/relation ratio (C/R R). AR is the average number of attributes per class. IR

TABLE 4.3

Metric-Based Evaluation of EO and TO

Metric	Attribute	EO	TO
Base	Axiom count (AC)	2,126	4,683
	Class count (CC)	272	261
	Data property count (DPC)	72	21
	Object property count (OPC)	17	22
	Individual count (IC)	220	929
Schema	Attribute richness (AR)	0.264706	0.08046
	Inheritance richness (IR)	1.191176	1.007663
	Relationship richness (RR)	0.1	0.226471
	Axiom/class ratio (A/C R)	7.816176	17.942529
	Inverse relation ratio (IRR)	0.022727	0.291667
	Class/relation ratio (C/R R)	0.755556	0.767647
Instance	Average population (AP)	0.808824	3.559387
	Class richness (CR)	0.150735	0.383142
Graph	Absolute root cardinality (ARC)	1	1
	Sibling cardinality (SC)	272	261
	Absolute leaf cardinality (ALC)	219	201
	Breadth	272	261
	Depth	1,129	1,299
Class (action in EO and armaments in TO)	Class importance (CI)	0.118182	0.217438
	Class readability (CR)	1	1
	Class instance count (CIC)	11	202

shows how well knowledge is organized into different groups and subgroups in the ontology. RR reflects the heterogeneity of the relationships in the ontology; it is calculated by dividing the number of non-inheritance relationships by the total number of relationships defined in the schema. A/C R represents the average amount of axioms per class. IRR is the ratio of inverse relations to total relations. C/R R is the ratio of classes to relations in the ontology.

- **Instance metric:** The instance metric evaluates how the specified knowledge is utilized, providing clues about the effectiveness of the ontology design. Two parameters are calculated: average population (AP) and class richness (CR). AP specifies the number of individuals as compared to the number of classes. CR indicates how instances are arranged across the classes, i.e., comparing between different classes.

- **Graph metric:** The graph metric evaluates the structure of the ontology according to parameters like absolute root cardinality (ARC), absolute leaf cardinality (ALC), sibling cardinality (SC), depth (D), and breadth (B).

- **Class metric:** The class metric examines the classes and relationships of the ontology by measuring class importance (CI), class readability (CR), and class instance count (CIC) for every class. For the EO, these metrics were measured for the class "Action"; for the TO, "Armaments."

4.3.1.2 Criteria-Based Evaluation

An ontology can be evaluated qualitatively according to the proposed criteria. OOPS! is one of the prominent criteria-based ontology evaluation tools. It classifies pitfalls (anomalies/errors) in the range P01 to P41 and emphasizes three types of errors: critical, important, and minor. Where critical errors need to be removed because they affect the reasoning process, important errors are not critical for any ontology function, but it is important to correct them. Minor errors do not represent any problem, but correcting them makes the ontology better and more user-friendly.

In evaluating EO and TO, three pitfalls were classified as important: P11 (Missing domain or range in properties), P24 (Using recursive definitions), and P30 (Equivalent classes not explicitly declared). Using OOPS!, five minor and two important pitfalls were reported in the EO; and four minor, two important, and one critical in the TO (see Table 4.4). The critical pitfall was permanently removed by enhancing the domain and range properties. All five minor pitfalls (P04, P07, P08, P13, and P21) were corrected accordingly with solutions such as adding annotations, declaring an inverse relationship, and following the naming conventions.

4.3.1.3 Cost-Based Evaluation

ONTOCOM is a significant tool used to detect the economic features of knowledge for the development of an ontology. Cost-based evaluation is done by measuring the development effort required to design the ontology. After ontology building, the development effort proceeds toward ontology maintenance and ontology reuse.

The total size of ontology development is calculated as

Size of Building (Size_B) + Size of Maintenance (Size_M) + Size of Reuse (Size_R).

The size of building is calculated as

$$\text{Size\_B} = (\text{concepts} + \text{relation} + \text{instances})/1000.$$

ONTOCOM has identified twenty effort multipliers (cost drivers) that have a rating level for statistical analysis. To predict the space complexity, five ratings from very low to very high are assigned to each cost driver, in the range of very low = 0.70 to very high = 1.60 for most. A high or very high rating of size indicates a complex modeled ontology having a high impact on the design effort. By contrast, low or very low indicates that the ontology modeled is simple in nature. The space complexity of the EO and TO was

TABLE 4.4

Criteria-Based Evaluation of EO and TO

Pitfall Number	Pitfall Description	Importance Level	Aspects	Elements Affected	Cases Detected in EO	Cases Detected in TO
P04	Creating unconnected ontology elements	Minor	Completeness	Classes, object and data properties	1	1
P07	Merging different concepts in the same class	Minor	Ontology Understanding	Concepts	8	7
P08	Missing annotations	Minor	Ontology clarity	Classes, object and data properties	302	358
P11	Missing domain or range in properties	Important	No inference	Object and data properties	31	—
P13	Inverse relationships not explicitly declared	Minor	No inference	Object properties	8	14
P19	Defining multiple domains or ranges in properties	Critical	Wrong Inference	Relationship and attributes	—	1
P21	Using a miscellaneous class	Minor	Modeling decisions	Classes	1	—
P24	Using recursive definitions	Important	Modeling decisions	Classes, object and data properties	—	1
P30	Equivalent classes not explicitly declared	Important	No inference	Classes	4	1

estimated by the size of the ontology to be designed and represented in various ontology primitives such as concepts, relations, instances, and axioms. There are 261 classes, 43 relations, and 4,683 axioms in the TO, and 272 classes, 89 relations, and 2,126 axioms in the EO. The size parameter of the estimation formula has been calculated as follows:

$$\text{Size of EO} = (272 + 89 + 2126)/1000 = 2.487 \text{kiloentities}$$
$$\text{Size of TO} = (261 + 43 + 4683)/1000 = 4.987 \text{kilentities}$$

According to the size, the rating is greater than the given scale for very high, which shows that both the modeled ontologies are heavyweight due to a large number of relations, axioms, and concepts.

4.3.2 Evaluation by Validation

The validation approach to evaluation of ontologies focuses on whether we are building the correct ontology. Usually, this is the only way to ensure the correctness of the knowledge encoded in the ontology. The validation of the EO and TO was carried out in two layers: semantic and application.

4.3.2.1 Semantic Layer

The semantic layer assesses whether all necessary data is included in the knowledge base and whether the ontology represents the domain sufficiently. It evaluates the semantic completeness, accuracy, conciseness, and correctness of the ontology. For this purpose, domain experts are involved in the evaluation.

Competency questions: The completeness of the ontology is evaluated by a set of competency questions, which are the most effective and reliable way to check whether all important information is included in the ontology. The ontology requirements are formulated as natural-language expressions for which the correct answers are provided. Translating the questions into formal SPARQL queries and evaluating them makes it simple to conclude what information is missing from the ontology and needs to be added. It must be remembered that competency questions are not an exhaustive qualitative measurement, and that even if all queries can be answered correctly, the ontology may still not be complete.

Various formal and informal competency questions covering the domain of emergency response were provided in natural language and translated into SPARQL queries. Each query was run on the ontology to test whether all requirements could be met and the correct answers inferred. For those queries that failed to run, the missing concepts or relations were added to the ontology. Nonetheless, the completeness of an ontology can never be proved, and constant enhancement is needed.

Expert interviews: For assessing the completeness of the ontology, domain experts are involved in the evaluation. Each expert receives a questionnaire specially developed for the domain and application of the ontology. Expert interviews can evaluate the completeness, accuracy, and conciseness of the classes and properties contained in the ontology. The experts are able to rate each answer and give additional remarks about the ontology to specify missing classes and properties or state redundancies.

Expert interviews were conducted to evaluate the completeness, correctness, and conciseness of the ontologies. A questionnaire containing twenty questions concerning the importance and clarity of each concept in the ontology was developed, so that domain experts in the field of emergency management could rate the ontologies and give additional feedback. By means of the received answers it was concluded which concepts were redundant, which were still missing, and which received the main focus.

4.3.2.2 Application Layer

The fitness of the ontology for its intended application can be assessed by using test cases and the ontology itself within the application. This is the last step of the evaluation and can only be done in the last stage of ontology development, when a finished ontology is available.

The effectiveness of the EO and TO was assessed by putting them to the real application they were designed to work for. Two use cases were used for this purpose: keyword search and visualization. The details of any concept in the EO or TO can be searched and responses generated in a time-bound manner. Both ontologies were visualized in tree and graph views. The visualization shows all the classes, subclasses, properties, and axioms. Keyword search provides an efficient search for any specific concept in the ontology. The EO and TO worked as expected.

The evaluation of the EO and TO indicated that the ontologies are well designed and suitable for the application. Only minor changes and adaptations to the lexical and structural layers were made. The validation of the ontologies revealed that most concepts relevant for the application were already included. Nonetheless, even after the evaluation it cannot be stated that the ontologies are fully complete, as they need constant improvement and adaptation during active usage.

4.4 Archiving Past Experiences (Case Base)

The case base, an integral part of the knowledge store, contains information from previous emergency situation cases. Emergency situation cases are described in terms of two vectors:

- **Feature Vector:** This is the specification of the emergency situation that can describe the important parameters from the point of view of a complicated case, to facilitate the retrieval of suitable emergency records. The parameter selection process was conducted by interactive discussion with a number of experts.

- **Action Vector:** This is a set of parameters that describe the problem's solution. It provides an emergency response solution consisting of emergency situation resources which may be required for relief, and the actions to be taken by the government or public. Resources include workers, medical aid, blankets, tents, vehicles, etc. Actions include assembling a rescue team, sending messages, developing an evacuation plan, etc.

4.5 Acquiring Expertise (Rule Base)

The rule base represents the logical relationship in the form of if-then statements, which allows for incremental development of knowledge representation. Ontology languages don't offer the expressivity we want. Rules are good at pluralistic relations with deductive knowledge, and there is interdependency among them. Experts' knowledge can be stored in the form of rules. Rules are created according to the following format:

[Description or Name of Rule: (conditions to be met) --> (facts to assert)]

Following are some of the sample rules in the rule base of the EKS.
    [1Actions:(?x rdf:type es:Earthquake), (?x es:has_location?l), (?x es:has_ magnitude?m),greaterThan(?m, 1.0),le(?m,2.0)->(?x es:needs_action es:H_L-1) (?x es:needs_action es:R_L-3)]
    [2Actions:(?x rdf:type es:Earthquake), (?x es:has_location?l), (?x es:has_ magnitude?m),greaterThan(?m, 2.0),le(?m,3.0)->(?x es:needs_action es:H_L-1) (?x es:needs_action es:R_L-2)]
    [3Actions:(?x rdf:type es:Earthquake), (?x es:has_location?l), (?x es:has_ magnitude?m),greaterThan(?m, 3.0),le(?m,4.0)->(?x es:needs_action es:H_L-1) (?x es:needs_action es:R_L-2)]
    [4Actions:(?x rdf:type es:Earthquake), (?x es:has_location?l), (?x es:has_ magnitude?m),greaterThan(?m, 4.0),le(?m,5.0)->(?x es:needs_action es:H_L-1) (?x es:needs_action es:R_L-2)]
    [5Actions:(?x rdf:type es:Earthquake), (?x es:has_location?l), (?x es:has_ magnitude?m),greaterThan(?m, 5.0),le(?m,6.0)->(?x es:needs_action es:H_L-1) (?x es:needs_action es:R_L-2)]
    [6Actions:(?x rdf:type es:Earthquake), (?x es:has_location?l), (?x es:has_ magnitude?m),greaterThan(?m, 6.0),le(?m,7.0)->(?x es:needs_action es:H_L-3) (?x es:needs_action es:R_L-3)]

[7Actions:(?x rdf:type es:Earthquake), (?x es:has_location?l), (?x es:has_magnitude?m),greaterThan(?m, 7.0),le(?m,8.0)->(?x es:needs_action es:H_L-4) (?x es:needs_action es:R_L-3)]

[8Actions:(?x rdf:type es:Earthquake), (?x es:has_location?l), (?x es:has_magnitude?m),greaterThan(?m, 8.0),le(?m,9.0)->(?x es:needs_action es:H_L-1) (?x es:needs_action es:R_L-2)]

[9Actions:(?x rdf:type es:Earthquake), (?x es:has_location?l), (?x es:has_magnitude?m),greaterThan(?m, 9.0),le(?m,10.0)->(?x es:needs_action es:H_L-1)(?x es:needs_action es:R_L-2)]

[r0:(?x es:has_location?y), (?y es:NbOfResidents?z) -> (?x es:NbOfPossible Victims?z)]

[r1:(?x rdf:type es:Ground_Shaking),(?x es:has_intensity?y), (?x es:has_location?c), (?c es:hasCriticalIntensity?I), greaterThan(?y,?I) -> (?x es:reaction IsNeeded "true")]

[r3:(?x rdf:type es:Ground_Shaking), (?x es:has_location?c), (?c es:has_primer_Landscape?l), (?l rdf:type es:Hilly) -> (?x es:needs_Prevention "true")]

[r4:(?x rdf:type es:Ground_Shaking), (?x es:reactionIsNeeded "true") -> (?x es:needs_Evacuation "true"), (?x es:needs_ClearingWork "true"),(?x es:needs_MedicalSupport "true"),(?x es:needs_SupplyGoodsSupport "true"), (?x es:needs_ClarificationOfSituation "true")]

[r5:(?x rdf:type es:Tornado), (?x es:has_distance_to_City?d), (?x es:has_speed?s), quotient(?d,?s,?c) -> (?x es:time_until_Event?c)]

[r6:(?x rdf:type es:Tornado), (?x es:time_until_Event?t), greaterThan(?t, 4) -> (?x es:needs_Evacuation "true")]

[r7:(?x rdf:type es:Tornado) -> (?x es:needs_SupplyGoodsSupport "true"), (?x es:needs_ClearingWork "true"), (?x es:needs_MedicalSupport "true"), (?x es:needs_EnlightenmentOfPopulation "true")]

[r8:(?x rdf:type es:Viral_Infectious_Diseases),(?x es:way_of_transmission "Air") -> (?x es:needs_Containment "true")]

[r9:(?x rdf:type es:Viral_Infectious_Diseases) -> (?x es:needs_MedicalSupport "true"), (?x es:needs_Prevention "true"), (?x es:needs_EnlightenmentOf Population "true")]

References

Adnan, Muhammad, and Muhammad Afzal. "Ontology based multiagent effort estimation system for scrum agile method." *IEEE Access* 5 (2017): 25993–26005.

Ait-Ameur, Yamine, Mickael Baron, Ladjel Bellatreche, Stephane Jean, and Eric Sardet. "Ontologies in engineering: the OntoDB/OntoQL platform." *Soft Computing* 21, no. 2 (2017): 369–389.

An, JungHyen, and Young B. Park. "Methodology for automatic ontology generation using database schema information." *Mobile Information Systems* 2018 (2018): 1359174.

Bilgin, Gozde, Irem Dikmen, and M. Talat Birgonul. "Ontology evaluation: an example of delay analysis." *Procedia Engineering* 85 (2014): 61–68.

Cheng, Haitao, Li Yan, Zongmin Ma, and Slobodan Ribaric. "Fuzzy spatio-temporal ontologies and formal construction based on fuzzy Petri nets." Computational Intelligence 35, no. 1 (2019): 204–239.

Chen, Wen-Hao, Yi Cai, Ho-Fung Leung, and Qing Li. "Generating ontologies with basic level concepts from folksonomies." Procedia Computer Science 1 no. 1 (2010): 573–581.

Corcho, Oscar, Mariano Fernández-López, and Asunción Gómez-Pérez. "Methodologies, tools and languages for building ontologies. Where is their meeting point?" *Data & Knowledge Engineering* 46, no. 1 (2003): 41–64.

Deaton, Chris, Blake Shepard, Charles Klein, Corrinne Mayans, Brett Summers, Antoine Brusseau, Michael Witbrock, et al. "The comprehensive Terrorism Knowledge Base in Cyc." In *Proceedings of the 2005 International Conference on Intelligence Analysis*, article 42. Publisher, 2005.

Ding, Fangyu, Quansheng Ge, Dong Jiang, Jingying Fu, and Mengmeng Hao. "Understanding the dynamics of terrorism events with multiple-discipline datasets and machine learning approach." *PLoS ONE* 12, no. 6 (2017): e0179057.

Ehrig Mark, and York Sure. "Ontology mapping – an integrated approach. In Bussler C.J., Davies J., Fensel D., and Studer R. (eds), The Semantic Web: Research and Applications. ESWS 2004. Lecture Notes in Computer Science, vol 3053. Springer, Berlin, Heidelberg, 2004. https://doi.org/10.1007/978-3-540-25956-5_6.

Ehrig, Mark, and Steffen Staab, "QOM-quick ontology mapping." Proceedings of the 3th International Semantic Web Conference, pp. 683–697. November 2004.

Ehrig, Mark, Steffen Staab, and York Sure. "Bootstrapping ontology alignment methods with APFEL." In Gil Y., Motta E., Benjamins V.R., and Musen M.A. (eds), The Semantic Web – ISWC 2005. ISWC 2005. Lecture Notes in Computer Science, Vol 3729. Springer, Berlin, Heidelberg, 2005. https://doi.org/10.1007/11574620_16.

Euzenat, Jérôme, and Pavel Shvaiko. Ontology Matching. Vol. 18. Springer, Heidelberg, 2007.

Farquhar, Adam, Richard Fikes, and James Rice. "The Ontolingua Server: a tool for collaborative ontology construction." *International Journal of Human-Computer Studies* 46, no. 6 (1997): 707–727.

Fellah, Aissa, Mimoun Malki, and Atilla Elci. "A similarity measure across ontologies for web services discovery." In *Web Services: Concepts, Methodologies, Tools, and Applications*, Vol. 138, pp. 859–881. IGI Global, 2019.

Gilbert, Emily. "Victim compensation for acts of terrorism and the limits of the state." *Critical Studies on Terrorism* 11, no. 2 (2018): 199–218.

Global Terrorism Index. Institute for Economics & Peace, Sydney, Australia, 2017. Available at http://visionofhumanity.org/app/uploads/2017/11/Global-Terrorism-Index-2017.pdf.

Guarino, Nicola, and Christopher A. Welty. "An overview of OntoClean." In *Handbook on ontologies*, pp. 151–171. Springer, Berlin, Germany, 2004.

Hooi, Yew Kwang, Mohd Fadzil Hassan, and Azmi M. Shariff. "A survey on ontology mapping techniques." In *Advances in Computer Science and Its Applications*, pp. 829–836. Springer, Berlin, Heidelberg, 2014.

Houghton, Brian K. "Terrorism Knowledge Base: a eulogy (2004–2008)." *Perspectives on Terrorism* 2, no. 7 (2008): 18–19.

Jain, Sarika, and Valerie Meyer. "Evaluation and refinement of emergency situation ontology." *International Journal of Information and Education Technology* 8, no. 10 (2018): 713–719.

Kalfoglou, Yannis, and Marco Schorlemmer. "Ontology mapping: the state of the art." The Knowledge Engineering Review 18, no. 1 (2003): 1–31.

Keet, C. Maria, Mari Carmen Suárez-Figueroa, and María Poveda-Villalón. "The current landscape of pitfalls in ontologies." In *Proceedings of the International Conference on Knowledge Engineering and Ontology Development (KEOD-2013)*, pp. 132–139. SciTePress, Setúbal, Portugal, 2013.

Knoke, David. "Emerging trends in social network analysis of terrorism and counterterrorism." In *Emerging Trends in the Social and Behavioral Sciences*, article 106. John Wiley & Sons, Hoboken, NJ, 2015.

Kotis, Konstantinos I., George A. Vouros, and Kostas Stergiou. "Towards automatic merging of domain ontologies: The HCONE-merge approach." Web Semant 4, no. 1 (2006): 60–79.

LaFree, Gary. "The Global Terrorism Database (GTD): accomplishments and challenges." *Perspectives on Terrorism* 4, no. 1 (2010): 24–46.

Lamurias, Andre, Diana Sousa, Luka A. Clarke, and Francisco M. Couto. "BOLSTM: classifying relations via long short-term memory networks along biomedical ontologies." *BMC Bioinformatics* 20, no. 1 (2019): 10.

Malik, Sonika, and Sarika Jain. "Sup_Ont: an upper ontology." *International Journal of Web-Based Learning and Teaching Technologies*, in press.

Mishra, Sanju, and Sarika Jain. "Automatic ontology acquisition and learning." *International Journal of Research in Engineering and Technology* 3, no. SI-14 (2014): 38–43.

Mohammadi, Majid, Wout Hofman, and Yao-Hua Tan. "Simulated annealing-based ontology matching." ACM Transactions on Management Information Systems (TMIS) 10, no. 1 (2019): 3.

Ngo, Duy Hoa, Zohra Bellahsene, and Remi Coletta. "Yam++-a combination of graph matching and machine learning approach to ontology alignment task." Journal of Web Semantics, 16, no. 16 (2012).

Niepert, Mathias, Cameron Buckner, and Colin Allen. "Answer set programming on expert feedback to populate and extend dynamic ontologies." In FLAIRS Conference, pp. 500–505. 2008.

Paredes-Moreno, Antonio, Francisco J. Martínez-López, and David G. Schwartz. "A methodology for the semi-automatic creation of data-driven detailed business ontologies." *Information Systems* 35, no. 7 (2010): 758–773.

Poveda-Villalón, María, Asunción Gómez-Pérez, and Mari Carmen Suárez-Figueroa. "OOPS! (OntOlogy Pitfall Scanner!): an on-line tool for ontology evaluation." *International Journal on Semantic Web and Information Systems* 10, no. 2 (2014): 7–34.

Qin, Yuchu, Wenlong Lu, Qunfen Qi, Xiaojun Liu, Meifa Huang, Paul J. Scott, and Xiangqian Jiang. "Towards an ontology-supported case-based reasoning approach for computer-aided tolerance specification." *Knowledge-Based Systems* 141 (2018): 129–147.

Salahi, Ahmed and Morteza Ansarinia. "Predicting network attacks using ontology-driven inference." arXiv preprint arXiv:1304.0913, 2013.

Schuurman, Bart. "Research on terrorism, 2007–2016: a review of data, methods, and authorship." *Terrorism and Political Violence* (2018): 1–16.

Soui, Makram, Soumya Diab, Ali Ouni, Aroua Essayeh, and Mourad Abed. "An ontology-based approach for user interface adaptation." In Advances in Intelligent Systems and Computing, pp. 199–215. Springer, Cham, 2017.

Staab, Steffen, and Rudi Studer (eds). Handbook on Ontologies. Springer Science & Business Media, 2010.

Staab, Steffen, Rudi Studer, Hans-Peter Schnurr, and York Sure. "Knowledge processes and ontologies." *IEEE Intelligent Systems* 16, no. 1 (2001): 26–34.

Wan, Jiafu, Boxing Yin, Di Li, Antonio Celesti, Fei Tao, and Qingsong Hua. "An ontology-based resource reconfiguration method for manufacturing cyber-physical systems." *IEEE/ASME Transactions on Mechatronics*, 23, no. 6 (2018): 2537–2546.

Welty, Christopher, and Nicola Guarino. "Supporting ontological analysis of taxonomic relationships." *Data & Knowledge Engineering* 39, no. 1 (2001): 51–74.

Wilkerson, Jerod, Tao Wang, Hsinchun Chen, and Robert P. Schumaker. "Terror Tracker System: a web portal for terrorism research." In *Proceedings of the 5th ACM/IEEE-CS Joint Conference on Digital Libraries (JCDL'05)*, pp. 416–416. IEEE, 2005.

Xue, Xingsi, and Jeng-Shyang Pan. "An overview on evolutionary algorithm based ontology matching." Journal of Information Hiding and Multimedia Signal Processing 9 (2018), 75–88.

Xue, Xingsi, and Yuping Wang. "Optimizing ontology alignments through a memetic algorithm using both matchfmeasure and unanimous improvement ratio." Artificial Intelligence 223 (2015): 65–81.

Xue, Xingsi, Yuping Wang, and Aihong Ren. "Optimizing ontology alignment through memetic algorithm based on partial reference alignment." Expert Systems with Applications 41, no. 7 (2014): 3213–3222.

Yap, Chee Een, and Myung Ho Kim. "Instance-based ontology matching with rough set features selection." In 2013 International Conference on IT Convergence and Security (ICITCS), pp. 1–4. IEEE. December 2013.

Zhang, Xing, and Guoping Xia. "A methodology for domain ontology construction based on Chinese technology documents." In Research and Practical Issues of Enterprise Information Systems II, pp. 1301–1310. Springer, Boston, MA, 2008.

5

Situation Awareness

The government, organizations, and the public need to prepare for the potential impacts of disasters. Ensuring that the necessary capabilities, resources, and knowledge are in place helps minimize the aftermath of these incidents. This chapter aims to develop an intelligent resource manager comprising a knowledge store along with procedures as a model for situation awareness to provide better interoperability of heterogeneous resources for emergency situation information. This resource manager supports end users in making the best decisions during an emergency by providing enhanced and real-time situation awareness to the general public [Jain and Patel 2019]. This resource manager is conceived as comprising ontological knowledge bases and use cases for contributing to the national effort of saving the nation and society in the face of emergencies. This system provides details of past incidents along with awareness for incoming emergencies in order to ensure the survival and continuity of services. With the help of this system, anyone in society will be able to contribute to the national effort of saving the nation when an emergency strikes that affects people as well as the economy.

5.1 System Architecture

Situation awareness is the perception, identification, and annotation of key elements semantically for comprehension of the situation at hand and projection of future status [Moreira et al. 2017]. Ontology representation facilitates efficient situation awareness by virtue of representing and storing information in a machine-understandable and interoperable format [Smart et al. 2007, Meditskos and Kompatsiaris 2017, van Heerden 2016, Malik and Jain 2017]. Emergency situation information is highly incomplete, scattered in various forms, and often not publicly available. The sources of such information are again dynamic and distinct. Emergency situations are very complex and unstructured, and have no single correct answer; they thus demand information integration and resource-management assistance that provide reasonable answers to a wide range of problems [Gupta et al. 2017, Jain and Patel 2020].

The system architecture of the resource manager is depicted in Figure 5.1. The system provides use cases for quickly visualizing and navigating any ontology in tree or graph view, generating a detailed description of some concept or keyword, and getting answers to questions posed. There are two ontologies created in Chapter 4 for the two types of emergencies under consideration: the earthquake ontology (EO) and terrorism ontology (TO).

Figure 5.1 shows all the components of the resource manager that comprise two major use cases, the Knowledge Base Browser and Question Answering module. The Knowledge Base Browser is designed with a focus on presenting keyword search results, metadata, and visualization on a single page that allows persistent results while the ontology is further explored. The Question Answering module provides inference over the data.

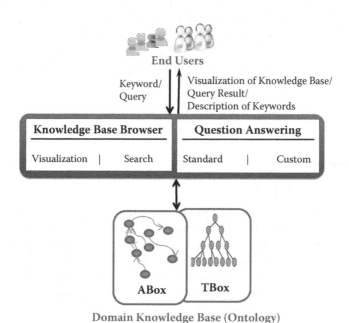

Domain Knowledge Base (Ontology)

FIGURE 5.1
Architecture of Resource Manager

5.2 Knowledge Base Browser

The Knowledge Base Browser allows the exploration of the contents of the ontology through appropriate visualizations. Both the use cases have been designed with the perspective of users who are not computer experts. The end user is not required to be familiar with any formal logic or query language. This panel also allows keyword search by clicking on the concept of the ontology.

5.2.1 Visualization

The Knowledge Base Browser allows the user to select the ontology for the domain of choice, and displays the contents either in a tree structure or graphically like a network. In tree view, the concepts are organized tax-onomically with nodes connected in a hierarchy, whereas in graph view the concepts are organized as in a semantic network, with nodes connected with all (taxonomic and non-taxonomic) relationships. It is possible to navigate through the concepts. Clicking on any concept results in a depiction of its detailed description. Visualizations of the ontology in tree and graph view, respectively, can be seen in Figures 5.2 and 5.3. The displayed

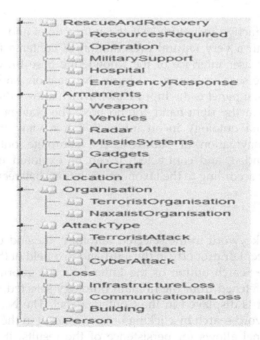

FIGURE 5.2
Tree View of Terrorism Ontology (TO)

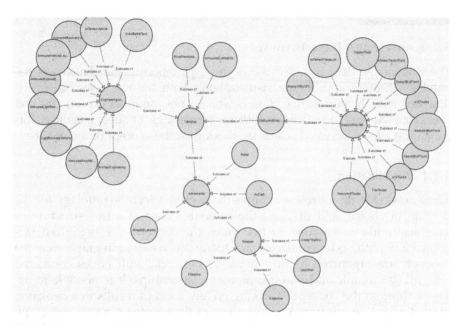

FIGURE 5.3
Graph View of Terrorism Ontology (TO)

ontology is interactive in nature. All the interactions and operations are very simple, with a very natural presentation of contents from a human perspective. The user interface of the Knowledge Base Browser has three panels, as can be seen in Figure 5.4: Input, Navigation, and Content. The topmost horizontal panel is the Input Panel, which allows the user to select the ontology from the right-hand combo box. The Navigation Panel displays the selected ontology in an interactive tree view that allows exploration and navigation of subtrees. The complete ontology can be navigated, expanded, and contracted. It can be explored from here in a hierarchical way according to the taxonomic relations between the concepts.

5.2.2 Search

To search for a keyword in the selected ontology, the end user enters the name of the concept or property in the left-hand text field of the Input Panel, then presses the Search button or the Enter key. All information for that concept will be fetched from the domain ontology selected. The output of the search result is displayed in the Content Panel. The Navigation Panel also allows keyword search by clicking on any concept in the tree structure. The Content Panel allows for persistence of the results; it houses search results, concept metadata, and descriptions of the relationships. Whenever a concept is entered into the search text field of the Input Panel or clicked in the tree structure of the Navigation Panel, its description is displayed in the Content Panel. The description includes the name of the concept, its description, related object properties, data properties, synonyms, relationships, and instances; where available, definitions will contain links out to the relevant resource. Figure 5.4 shows the description of the concept "Organization," which was entered into the search text box. It displays the description, synonyms, superclass, subclasses, domain, range, and instances of the concept.

This search module provides semantic rather than syntactic search, because it searches the concept from the ontology according to the meaning that is encoded by classification of the features of an entity. A user can search the same concept by inputting its synonyms, which will be provided to the SPARQL query by a regular expression. These features provide a semantic linkage between the concepts rather than keyword-based matching. The procedure of the keyword search follows:

Input Keyword Y

Using Jena library do the following

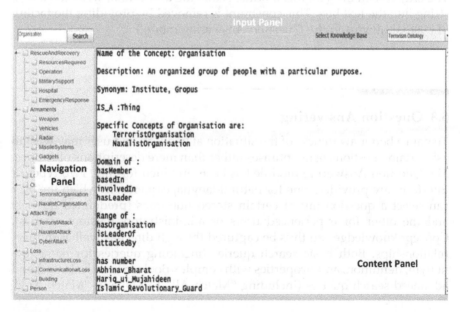

FIGURE 5.4
The Knowledge Base Browser

a. *Fetch description of keyword Y*
"Select?Comment WHERE {ns:"+ Y +" rdfs:comment?Comment."+"}"

b. *Fetch synonym of keyword Y*
"Select?Subject WHERE {?Subject rdfs:isDefinedBy?a. FILTER (regex (str(?a), "Y"))"

c. *Fetch superclass of keyword Y*
"SELECT?SuperClass WHERE {ns:" + Y +" rdfs:subClassOf?SuperClass. "+"}");

d. *Fetch subclasses of keyword Y*
"Select?Subclasses WHERE {?Subclasses rdfs:subClassOf ns:"+ Y +".}"

e. *Fetch domain of keyword Y*
"Select?Subject" + "WHERE {?Subject rdfs:domain ns:"+ Y +".}"

f. *Fetch range of keyword Y*
"Select?Subject" + "WHERE {?Subject rdfs:range ns:"+ Y +".}"

g. *Fetch instances of keyword Y*
"Select *{?hasNumber rdf:type ns:"+ Y +"."+"}"

Display the Results

The Knowledge Base Browser provides an interface for the user to browse the knowledge which is stored in the domain ontologies. The user writes a concept in natural language and fetches relevant information semantically. The only constraint with this module is that the user cannot write too long a string into the text box. This constraint is removed by providing the facility of custom queries in the Question Answering module.

5.3 Question Answering

To gain a better awareness of the situation at hand, an end user may wish to ask certain questions using phrases rather than mere descriptions of entities. The Question Answering module has been provided for this. Two types of interfaces are provided, one for natural-language queries in which the user can select a question out of certain stored questions (predefined queries) and the other for experienced users or administrators (custom queries). Concept knowledge can thus be captured through direct as well as indirect relationships. Both basic search queries (including queries for name, synonym, definition, and properties with complex Boolean search strings) and advanced search queries (including "Match All" [AND] and "Match Any"

[OR]) are supported. Both predefined and custom queries are demonstrated on the TO.

5.3.1 Predefined Queries

Predefined queries in English providing general awareness to the public were selected after discussion with the stakeholders. Two broad ranges of queries have been incorporated:

1. The first type provides details related to the availability of resources, services provided by the government in order to make military personnel ready for any mishap, and regiments existing today, along with related details (location, year of establishment, motto, etc.).

2. The second type defines events of the past with details like how the event took place and what effects it had on our society by providing the number of casualties, infrastructural damage, etc. For the earthquake domain, this type of query provides details like which non-governmental organizations helped the most in some incident and the number of earthquakes with a given location, magnitude, etc. For the terrorism domain, this type of query provides details like the weapons used by the attackers, the number of attacks by state, the number of attacks perpetrated by different organizations, etc.

Table 5.1 lists some selected queries over the TO and their SPARQL counterparts based on the different types of SPARQL constructs used to write them.

Figure 5.5 shows the user interface for predefined queries and the results after executing query number 6 of the interface. The left-hand side panel displays the list of queries over the TO. The right-hand side panel displays the results of executing the queries.

These natural-language queries present a clear, concise, and accurate view of potential events and discuss a general concept of operations for response. Dynamic combo boxes have been used in this interface. Presuming that the ontology will grow and include as much information as possible that is unique to response actions, updated information will be displayed in the combo box. The updated ontology information will also be reflected in the output of standard queries. Our system provides real-time information due to its non-monotonic nature. Non-monotonicity is required for the open-world assumption, because if information is updated, then output should be displayed according to the updated information. With the help of

TABLE 5.1

Predefined Queries over the TO

SN	Natural-Language Query	SPARQL Query
1	Display total casualties (deaths and injuries) by state.	"SELECT?State (SUM(?Death) as?Dead) (SUM(?injury) as?Injured)\n" + "WHERE {?Attack my:attackedAt?City.\n" + "?City my:isPartOf?State.\n" + "?Attack my:numberOfPersonsInjured?injury.\n" + "?Attack my:numberOfPersonsDied?Death.}\n" +"GROUP BY?State";
2	Display the total number of attacks by state.	"SELECT?State (count(?City) as?Count)\n" + "WHERE {?Attack rdf:type my:TerroristAttack.\n" + "?Attack my:attackedAt?City.\n" + "?City my:isPartOf?State.} \n" + "Group by?State";
3	Display total casualties by terrorist organization.	"SELECT?Organisation (SUM(?Death) as?totaldeath)\n" + "WHERE {?Attack my:attackedBy?Organisation.\n" + "?Attack my:numberOfPersonsDied?Death.} \n" + "Group by?Organisation";
4	Display attack and its description by state.	"SELECT distinct?Attack?Description\n" + "WHERE {?Attack rdf:type my:TerroristAttack.\n" + "?Attack my:attackedAt?City.\n" + "?City my:isPartOf my:"+ state +".\n" + "optional{?Attack my:hasDescription?Description }} ";
5	Display name of attack that had greatest number of casualties.	"SELECT distinct *\n" + "WHERE {?Attack rdf:type my:TerroristAttack.\n" + "?Attack my:numberOfPersonsDied?Casualties.}\n" + "ORDER BY DESC(?casualties) LIMIT 1";
6	Display all operations been taken by Indian forces per year.	"SELECT?Operation\n" + "where {?Operation rdf:type my:Operation.\n" + "?Operation my:hasStartDate?Date." + "FILTER (?Date >= \"" + Integer.toString(Integer.parseInt(year)) + "-01-01T00:00:00\"^^xsd:dateTime &&?Date < \"" + Integer.toString(Integer.parseInt(year) + 1) + "-01-01T00:00:00\"^^xsd:dateTime).}\n";
7	Display the names of regiments according to seniority level.	"SELECT?Regiment\n" + "WHERE{?Regiment rdf:type my:InfantryRegiment.\n" + "?Regiment my:seniorityRank?seniority}\n" + "order by (?seniority)";

knowledge analytics, the resource manager also provides all updated resources. For example: Suppose the total number of types of missile used to date by the Indian Army is ten. If, in the future, India—alone or with the collaboration of another country—develops a new missile, then the newly developed missile will be stored in the ontology either manually or automatically, along with how it works.

The interface shows three panels. The left panel "Select Ontology" lists predefined queries:

Select Ontology	Terrorism Ontology	
1. Death and injury state wise for test ets etste st		Execute
2. Attacks done by	Abhinav_Bharat	
3. Number of terrorist attacks based on states.		Execute
4. Killed or injured till date state wise.		Execute
5. Number of maoist attacks based on states.		Execute
6. Name of attack with weapons used		Execute
7. Total deaths caused by different organisation		Execute
8. Attack and description in the state	Assam	
9. Attack with most number of casualties		Execute
10. Attack with compensation details		Execute
11. Operations taken year wise	1948	
12. Description of	Operation_All_Out	
13. Casualties of	Operation_All_Out	
14. Fought between detail of	Operation_All_Out	
15. Workshop location and responsibility	505_ABW	Execute
16. Regiments based on their seniority level		
17. Regiment Location and their establishment year	Parachute_Regiment	
18. Regiment motto	Parachute_Regiment	
19. Branches of Regiment	ArmouredRegiment	

The right panel "Query Type - Standard":

Attack	Weapon
SamjhautaExpress2007	Bomb
Ayodhya2005	Grenade
Ayodhya2005	M1911
Ayodhya2005	Type56
IndianParliament2001	Pistol
IndianParliament2001	AK47
IndianParliament2001	Grenade
Jaipur2008	Bomb
Kilenar2018	Gun
Kilenar2018	Bomb
MahabodhiTemple2013	IED
MahabodhiTemple2013	CylinderBombs
Delhi2008	Bomb
Agartala2008	Bomb
Bangaluru2008	Bomb
MeccaMasjid2007	Cyclotol
Mumbai2008	IED
Mumbai2008	AK47
Mumbai2008	Grenade
Mumbai2008	RDX
Gurudaspur2015	NightVisionDevices
Gurudaspur2015	AK47
Gurudaspur2015	GPSDevice
Gurudaspur2015	Grenade
GermanBakery2010	IED
BalajanTiniali2016	AK56
BalajanTiniali2016	Grenade
BalajanTiniali2016	AK47
CRPFPulwama2017	Grenade

FIGURE 5.5
Predefined Queries

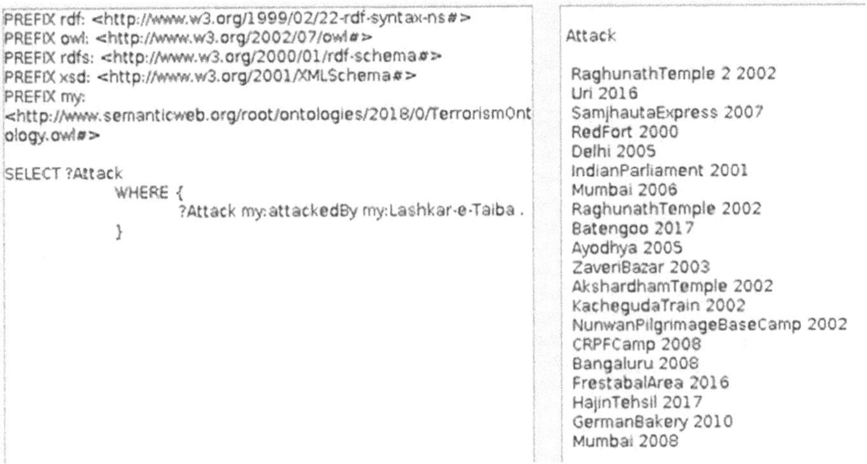

```
PREFIX rdf: <http://www.w3.org/1999/02/22-rdf-syntax-ns#>
PREFIX owl: <http://www.w3.org/2002/07/owl#>
PREFIX rdfs: <http://www.w3.org/2000/01/rdf-schema#>
PREFIX xsd: <http://www.w3.org/2001/XMLSchema#>
PREFIX my:
<http://www.semanticweb.org/root/ontologies/2018/0/TerrorismOnt
ology.owl#>

SELECT ?Attack
         WHERE {
             ?Attack my:attackedBy my:Lashkar-e-Taiba .
         }
```

```
Attack

RaghunathTemple 2 2002
Uri 2016
SamjhautaExpress 2007
RedFort 2000
Delhi 2005
IndianParliament 2001
Mumbai 2006
RaghunathTemple 2002
Batengoo 2017
Ayodhya 2005
ZaveriBazar 2003
AkshardhamTemple 2002
KachegudaTrain 2002
NunwanPilgrimageBaseCamp 2002
CRPFCamp 2008
Bangaluru 2008
FrestabalArea 2016
HajinTehsil 2017
GermanBakery 2010
Mumbai 2008
```

FIGURE 5.6
Custom Queries

5.3.2 Custom Queries

Though the questions stored as predefined queries should fulfill the needs of an average user, an advanced interface is provided for custom queries (Figure 5.6). The user can enter the desired SPARQL query in the left-hand panel, and the result is displayed in the right-hand panel. Figure 5.6 shows the result of attacks done by Lashkar-e-Taiba. The only constraint with this module is that the user has to provide the query in SPARQL.

References

Gupta, Chhavi, Amit Bhardwaj, Sanju Mishra, and Sarika Jain. "A semantic web portal for unconventional emergencies." In *2017 8th International Conference on Computing, Communication and Networking Technologies (ICCCNT)*, pp. 1–4. IEEE, 2017.

Jain, Sarika, and Archana Patel. "Smart ontology-based event identification." In *2019 IEEE 13th International Symposium on Embedded Multicore/Many-core Systems-on-Chip (MCSoC)*, pp. 135–142. IEEE, 2019.

Jain, Sarika, and Archana Patel. "Situation-aware decision-support during man-made emergencies." In *Proceedings of ICETIT 2019*, pp. 532–542. Springer, Cham, Switzerland, 2020.

Malik, Sonika, and Sarika Jain. "Ontology based context aware model." In *2017 International Conference on Computational Intelligence in Data Science (ICCIDS)*, pp. 1–6. IEEE, 2017.

Meditskos, Georgios, and Ioannis Kompatsiaris. "iKnow: ontology-driven situational awareness for the recognition of activities of daily living." *Pervasive and Mobile Computing* 40 (2017): 17–41.

Moreira, João Lqiz Rebelo, Luís Ferreira Pires, Marten van Sinderen, and Patricia Dockhorn Costa. "Ontology-driven conceptual modeling for early warning systems: redesigning the Situation Modeling Language." In *Proceedings of the 5th International Conference on Model-Driven Engineering and Software Development (MODELSWARD 2017)*, pp. 467–477. SciTePress, Setúbal, Portugal, 2017.

Smart, Paul R., Alistair Russell, Nigel R. Shadbolt, M. C. Shraefel, and Leslie A. Carr. "AKTiveSA." *The Computer Journal* 50, no. 6 (2007): 703–716.

van Heerden, Renier, Peter Chan, Louise Leenen, and Jacques Theron. "Using an ontology for network attack planning." *International Journal of Cyber Warfare and Terrorism* 6, no. 3 (2016): 65–78.

6

Advisory System

A semantics-based DSS can solve most of the problems associated with a plain DSS. This chapter focuses on best practices—i.e., decision trees, ontological representation, case-based and rule-based reasoning—and demonstrates an ontology-supported hybrid reasoning framework for generating advice. As in the previous chapter, an emergency domain—in this case earthquakes—has been chosen to demonstrate the applicability of the integrated approach. A case base of past earthquakes is created with ontological representation and recommendations generated by its real-time synthesis and matching with the input earthquake data using decision-tree classification. The rule base serves as expert advice in case of a similarity mismatch with all historical cases. This framework generates recommendations with proper justification based on past experiences and experts' codified knowledge. It can support decision makers and emergency managers by providing an overview of the current situation and generating a rapid automated action plan within a time constraint, which can be further validated by an expert. The system has been tested on the domain of earthquakes and can work for any emergency situation whose domain knowledge is entered into it.

6.1 Conceptual Model

Various techniques have been utilized in planning and recommendation [Sehgal et al. 2016]. The two most utilized knowledge-based methods are case-based reasoning (CBR) and rule-based reasoning (RBR). No single method used in isolation achieves the desired results.

- When only the case base is used, without any other explicit knowledge, CBR is no better than a plain database retrieval system using SQL queries or a nearest-neighbor classifier. Such a system is not able to exploit the full powers of CBR, as it is performing

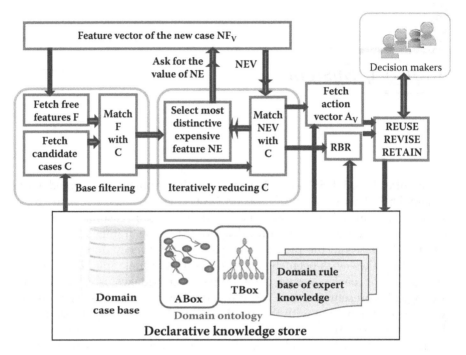

FIGURE 6.1
Knowledge-Driven Situation Awareness and Advisory Support (KDSAAS)

similarity search and retrieval based upon case-by-case search of the complete case base [Papadopoulos 2018, Chakraborty 2010].

- When used alone, RBR encounters problems for domains that are broad and complex, those where knowledge cannot be represented in the form of rules (i.e., IF-THEN), and those where knowledge evolves rapidly. As experts are a scarce resource, knowledge acquisition is also a bottleneck. RBR systems may prove to be unreliable and sometimes brittle, because even one faulty rule can considerably affect the whole system's performance. Updating such RBR systems and proving their consistency is expensive.

Integrated approaches have demonstrated their effectiveness in many application areas (like planning, diagnosis, and recommendation) and various domains of study (like medicine, agriculture, banking, and emergencies) [Sahebjamnia et al. 2017]. The limitations of an individual method can be removed or at least lightened by the use of complementary methods. Knowledge-driven situation awareness and advisory support (KDSAAS) uses CBR augmented with semantic technologies, decision trees, and rules for deducing recommendations in the state of emergency (see Figure 6.1).

CBR is one of the most popular techniques for recommendation based on historical cases.

KDSAAS presents a hybrid approach to reasoning; each component complements the other ones. CBR is the basis and provides the basic course. Decision trees and RBR augment the retrieval phase of CBR. Decision trees help in filtering and reducing the search space. If no historical case in the case base matches the input case, RBR acts as an expert to provide advice. Ontologies are utilized for case representation and storage, which allows semantic representation of the case base and makes the general domain knowledge explicit. Through augmenting the hybrid approach with the ontological representation, more flexible and contextual reasoning can be achieved [Zhang et al. 2016, Xu et al. 2014, Onorati et al. 2014, Li et al. 2008, Masuwa-Morgan and Burrell 2004, Haghighi et al. 2013, Malizia et al. 2010, Han and Xu 2015].

6.1.1 Algorithmic Overview

Following is the algorithmic overview for this hybrid approach. The details of each component follow in subsequent sections. The stored knowledge comprises the case base and the rule base. The algorithm assumes that the domain ontology has already been created with the process discussed in Chapter 4. The individuals in this ontology serve as the case base. The rule base is created in collaboration with domain experts. The control enters into the system via the DOR-CBR() algorithm. The CBR proceeds with its four life-cycle stages: retrieve, reuse, revise, and retain. The algorithm explains the augmentation of this basic CBR algorithm with semantic technologies (signified by O in DOR-CBR), decision-tree classification (signified by D in DOR-CBR), and RBR (signified by R in DOR-CBR).

Knowledge Store
> Ontology as the Case Base
> Rule Base   // Rule Base is described by R ($R_1, R_2, R_3, ... R_n$)

Input
> Feature Vector of the New Case ($NF_V = \{f_1, f_2, f_3, ..., f_f\}$) in case of O-CBR
> Feature Vector of the free features of the New Case in case of DO-CBR

Output
> List of Actions (NA_V)

DOR-CBR()

// Stage 1: RETRIEVE

Call O-Retrieve OR DO-Retrieve   // Fetch the most similar case

If ((S_m>=Threshold for O-Retrieve) OR (Candidate set is not null for DO-Retrieve))

$A_V \leftarrow$ Fetch the list of actions of C_m from the Ontology.
Else $A_V \leftarrow$ RBR (NF_V)   // Switch to RBR
// Stage 2: REUSE
Recommend A_v to the operator.
// Stage 3: REVISE or ADAPT
$NA_V \leftarrow$ Operator decides upon the final list of actions
$N_C \leftarrow NF_V, NA_V$
// Stage 4: RETAIN
Retain N_C to case base as a new case.
Exit.

6.2 Case-Based Reasoning

Humans gain competence in problem solving as they base their reasoning on examples and past experiences. Similarly, the reasoning in knowledge-based systems often benefits from the use of CBR. CBR proceeds on the basis of recollecting past events and observations and utilizing these experiences to solve the situation at hand by exploiting similarity measures; successful solutions are stored for later use. Previously solved and memorized pieces of knowledge or problem situations are called cases.

6.2.1 Representation and Storage of Cases

The case structure consists mainly of two parts, the features of the problem (e.g., symptoms of a disease or attributes of an earthquake) and the solution class (e.g., a diagnosis of a disease or an action to be taken during an earthquake). Based on the logical structure of cases, there are different ways of representing them, including traditional feature-vector methods; AI formalisms of representation such as semantic nets, frames, predicates, objects, and rules; and the semantic knowledge-intensive method of ontologies. Cases can be stored physically in flat files, databases (relational, object-oriented, or graph databases), or XML files.

6.2.2 CBR Life Cycle

The CBR life cycle has basically four processing stages:

- Retrieve (to fetch the most similar case),

- Reuse (to utilize this retrieved case in solving the current problem),
- Revise (to adapt or repair the case if required),
- Retain (to save the input case as a new case in the case base).

Of the four stages, retrieval is the most significant and focuses on fetching the most similar case from all the stored cases in the case base. Various similarity measures have been devised and employed for case retrieval, such as cosine similarity, Canberra distance, Euclidean distance, squared chord distance, Manhattan distance, and Hamming distance. CBR then attempts to reuse the fetched most similar case, i.e., apply its solution to the problem at hand. The proposed solution may need to be adapted, repaired, or revised according to the input case. The new input case, along with the proposed (revised) solution is retained as a new case in the case base for future reference. In the retain stage, accumulation and storage of successful cases in the case base continuously improves the ability of the CBR system to solve problems.

6.3 Augmenting CBR with Semantic Technologies

Though traditional CBR systems have enjoyed considerable success in different application domains, they lack an understanding of the semantic structure of cases, which is very important for intelligent knowledge retrieval in decision support system. Semantic technologies play an important role in capturing, structuring, sharing, and reusing knowledge, thereby enhancing the capabilities of CBR systems [Amailef and Lu 2013, Qin et al. 2018, Zhu et al. 2018]. Ontologies can serve as an efficient tool for case representation and storage, case indexing and retrieval, case revision, and case retention. Augmenting CBR with ontologies solves the knowledge-acquisition bottleneck by allowing semantic representation of the case base and discover of cases from already-existing domain ontologies. These knowledge-intensive CBR systems are able to reason with semantic, more realistic, and practical criteria rather than purely syntactic ones. Ontologies make the general domain knowledge explicit, facilitating CBR in reasoning more flexibly and contextually. The CBR decision-making process reaps the following benefits from ontological representation:

- **General Applicability:** The ontology can store information about different concepts under one roof and with different level of details.
- **High Flexibility and Expandability:** The ontological case base has the flexibility of updating and expanding itself like human memory.
- **Machine Understandable:** Because of the ontology-based semantic

representation, the knowledge base becomes machine under-standable and processable.

- **Highly Distributed:** Because of its semantic interoperability and consistent knowledge expression, the processes of building a knowledge base by experts and providing decision support to users can be highly distributed. Therefore, an ontology promotes knowledge integration and sharing by ensuring the accumulation, integration, reuse, sharing, and management of knowledge in a seamless manner.

- **Concept matching:** Ontologies facilitate CBR by enhancing the concept matching process. Various ontology matching algorithms may be utilized for the purpose.

- **Heterogeneous Cases:** Cases may not share the same characteristics or features. Ontological representation is powerful in handling case similarity in such scenarios.

- **System Reuse:** The common representation language used allows the CBR system to be reused in other domains and even to inter-operate with other non-CBR-based systems.

Some noteworthy CBR systems utilizing semantic technologies include Alexia, Manomia, Care-Partner, and Mémoire.

6.3.1 Life Cycle of Ontology-Based CBR

Ontology-based CBR utilizes the semantic knowledge-intensive method of representing cases in the case base. Knowledge-intensive methods incorporate domain ontology with necessary semantic relations for case representation. The utilization of ontology for case representation enhances every stage of CBR, from retrieval to retention. During the retrieval stage, traditional CBR systems disregard the variety of different cases and the semantic relationships between concepts. Ontology-based CBR focuses on the semantic relations while performing case retrieval and proves to be better in both quantity and quality than its traditional counterpart.

In an ontology-based case representation, every instance (individual) represents a specialized case. The cases are captured as instances of classes. After knowledge acquisition from varied sources, the resulting case base is heterogeneous in nature, with possibly different attributes for different cases. The problems of heterogeneity are solved by dynamic representation of cases and ontology matching. Various ontology instance-matching approaches have been proposed in the literature and can be utilized in ontology-based CBR as well. In addition to retrieving the most similar case quickly and accurately, the ontology-based approach facilitates all aspects of semantic case retrieval. Now the similarity between two cases is judged not only on the basis of their features but also on their relation with other cases and their structure. Similarity between two cases is based on data and object properties of the instances involved, the classes they are instances of, and the classes they are inherited from higher in the hierarchy.

For simplicity, this case study utilizes a homogeneous case base by involving instances only of earthquakes. In the emergency case study, the attributes location and magnitude are considered for calculating the similarity of two earthquakes. The weight of each attribute of every class and individual is elicited in a manner such that the summation of all weights should be 1. The similarity measure depends on the measuring scale of each attribute. There are two types of attributes in the earthquake ontology, those with numeric values and those with string values. For string values, the attributes take values from a constrained list.

If x_i is the value of attribute i for case x and y_i is the value of attribute i for case y, the string similarity value $SSim(x_i, y_i)$ of the attributes of cases x and y is calculated for each string attribute i using the following equation:

$$SSim(xi, \; yi) \; = \; \begin{cases} 1, \; if \; xi = yi, \\ 0, \; if \; xi \neq yi \end{cases} \tag{1}$$

The numeric similarity value $NSim(x_i, y_i)$ of the attributes of cases x and y is calculated for each numeric attribute i using the following equation:

$$NSim(xi, \; yi) = \frac{min(xi, \; yi)}{max(xi, \; yi)} \tag{2}$$

The total similarity $Sim(x, y)$ between cases x and y, incorporating all string and numeric attributes, is the weighted average, calculated as

$$Sim(x, \; y) = \frac{\Sigma \, (wi * Sim(xi, \; yi))}{N} \times 100 \tag{3}$$

where $Sim(x_i, y_i)$ can be the SSim or the NSim based on the data type of x_i and y_i, and N is the total number of attributes.

```
// Ontology-based Case Retrieval Cₘ, Sₘ←O-Retrieve (NFᵥ)
Knowledge Store
    Ontology as the case base with the candidate set of cases C = {C₁, C₂, ..., Cᵪ}
Input
    Feature vector of the new case, NFᵥ = {f₁, f₂, f₃, ..., fᵩ}
Output
    The most similar case Cₘ and the similarity value Sₘ
```

O-Retrieve()

$Sm \leftarrow 0$

C ←Fetch all the instances (along with their feature vectors) of the concept from the ontology pertaining to which recommendations are required. // E.g., instances of the concept "Earthquake."

c← No. of such instances received. These are the historical cases.

for each case $C_i(0<=i<=c)$ // The candidate set has c cases

        $f_i \leftarrow$ feature vector of C_i

        for each feature $f_{ij}(0<=j<=f)$ of $C_i$do   // Every case has f features

                if f_{ij}(data-type) = numeric then eq←eq2

                else if f_{ij}(data-type) = string eq← eq1

                $S_j \leftarrow eq(f_{ij}, f_j)$ // Create the similarity vector of case C_i

        Current Similarity (C_s) ←eq3 (S_v, W_v)

        if $(C_s>S_m)$ $S_m \leftarrow C_s$ and count ←i

$C_m \leftarrow C_i$

6.4 Augmenting CBR with Decision Trees

One problem with using standard CBR methodology is that it requires complete description and specification of the input case in order to perform case retrieval, which is often impractical in many domains, such as disease diagnosis and natural disasters. A full case description (all the features and attributes) may not be available, or may be expensive to procure at the beginning of the reasoning process, with the exception of a very small set of starting basic features that are available freely at the outset.

6.4.1 Incremental CBR

To address this issue, the CBR approach is augmented with a decision-tree classification approach that initiates case retrieval with only a skeletal case description (consisting of only the basic available features) and obtains the extra discriminating information during the process. The features representing any case in a CBR system are classified into free features (readily available) and expensive features (not readily available). This Incremental case-based reasoning CBR is characterized by and benefits from the fact that of the expensive features, the values of only some are actually required to find the most similar case; the rest of the features are not required at all. Expensive features are asked for as and when needed. In fact, free features plus a subset of expensive features are adequate for case retrieval. The Incremental CBR approach can be used in situations where finding similarity with a huge number of features is expensive and time consuming and where not all the features of the input case are readily available to trigger case retrieval in CBR. The Incremental CBR approach has two components:

1. **Base Filtering:** The first key component of Incremental CBR is the building of the initial candidate set. It involves identifying a subset of relevant candidate cases by using free features. A set of cases possibly matching the input case is rapidly identified based on free features, and the most incompatible cases are filtered out. A flat search over the case base could be performed for cases which match the free features with the values of the input case. Alternatively, another level of traditional CBR could be utilized for this purpose. The matching threshold can be fixed; it can be a 100% match during the base filtering, or looser selection criteria can be adopted as appropriate in some situations. The result of this component is a reduced set of cases from the case base which serve as relevant candidate cases for the next component.

2. **Iteratively Reducing the Candidate Set:** The next component of Incremental CBR is identifying a minimal set of expensive features (using the relevant candidate cases) when, when instantiated with the input case values, will lead to sufficient information to reach to the most similar case. This component of Incremental CBR is iterative in nature, with each iteration comprising three steps. At each iteration, the most distinctive feature (DF) is selected out of the remaining features (step 1); its value for the input case is demanded by the user (step 2); and it is matched for each case in the current candidate set of cases (step 3). The cases whose current selected DF does not match the input case are discarded from the candidate set of cases, in effect narrowing down the set of candidate cases. For some cases, the value of this current most DF may be unknown; these cases may be allowed to remain in the candidate set. The termination of this component depends on the trade-off between the availability of expensive features and the time left to declare the result of recommendation.
   Terminating: Either the features are exhausted, i.e., the leaf node of the decision tree is reached (as will be discussed in the next section), or the value of the current most DF is not available for the input case.

```
// Decision Tree and Ontology-Augmented CBR
DO-Retrieve()
// Component 1: Base Filtering
Identify the free features
Free ← Input the values of free features for the new case.
```

C ←Fetch all instances (along with their feature vectors) of the concept from the ontology pertaining to which recommendations are required.

c← No. of such instances received. These are the historical cases.

count← 0

for each case $C_i(0<=i<=c)$ // The candidate set has c cases

       if the value of some free feature of new case does not match the value of that feature of C_i

            C ←C – C_i // Remove that case from the candidate set

            count++

c = c-count

Now the candidate set has c cases.

// **Component 2: Iteratively Reducing the Candidate Set**

Repeat the following until the set of expensive features is exhausted OR the value of the next most expensive feature for the new case is not available:

NE ← Select the next most distinctive expensive feature

NEV ← Input the value of NE for the new case.

for each case $C_i(0<=i<=c)$ // Narrow down the set of candidate cases.

       if the value of NE of C_i does not match NEV

            C ←C – C_i // Remove that case from the candidate set

            c--   // Decrement 1 from the number of candidate sets

6.4.2 Selecting the Most Distinctive Feature

The process of selecting the most DF is best explained by constructing a decision tree. The tree will be minimal if the feature selected to designate the nodes starting from the root has the most discriminatory power at that level, meaning that it is the most DF out of the set of features. This decision tree will have leaf nodes that correspond to different solution classes (different types of cases). One solution class corresponds to one set of actions or diagnosis for the set of cases located at this leaf node. The internal nodes of the decision tree correspond to the features. Similar cases fall into one solution class, i.e., the set of cases will be classified, or are located on the leaf nodes. Each leaf node may contain some cases that fall into the solution class corresponding to it. The features providing the most information should be planned high up in the tree (close to the root). We need to find a means of measuring the information content of case features to identify their discriminatory power with respect to the solution classes. The ID3 algorithm is one such means. Using this algorithm, the most distinctive expensive feature is chosen at each level. The next level is partitioned into the values of the selected feature.

Consider three sets. The first set is the set of expensive features $F = \{f_1, f_2, ..., f_f\}$ that will reside at the internal nodes of the decision tree constructed.

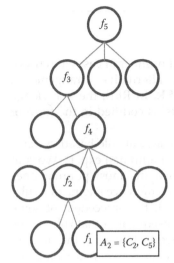

FIGURE 6.2
Selecting the Most Distinctive Feature

The second set is the complete list of cases C = {C_1, ..., C_c} to be classified. The third set is the set of possible solution classes or case categories or actions A = {A_1, ..., A_a}, which will form the leaves of the decision tree. Every action A_i will correspond to one or more cases in C; let $|A_i|$ be the number of cases with action A_i. Any information emanating from the root of the decision tree thus constructed will reach to one of the solution classes or action messages from the set A.

Every internal node partitions the set of cases on it into a further n groups based on the n different values of the feature residing on that internal node. Let the internal node representing feature f have n possible values {v_1, v_2, ..., v_n}; then this node will have n branches such that branch B_i corresponds to those cases that have value v_i for feature f. Say f_5 is the most DF at the root (Figure 6.2). This feature can have three values, so the case set is divided into three groups. Then f_3 is selected, and finally f_1, which has two cases C_2 and C_5 in this solution class.

In the ID3 algorithm, a global decision tree is constructed over the entire set of cases; in contrast, here a partial and local decision tree is constructed every time over the reduced set of relevant candidate cases. Thus, there is a consistent reduction in the number of features used for determining the action. This is possible due to the fact that no global decision tree exists that is general for all inputs. Instead, a local decision tree is constructed that is specific to the input case and considerably more efficient. Moreover, the general decision tree would have to be constructed over the entire feature set; this local tree is very compact, as it is free of free features and also those features with less discriminatory power. In fact, the decision tree constructed is just logical rather than actually built; instead, some leaf node is reached by tracing a single path from the root.

6.5 Augmenting CBR with Rules

At times, the case base does not have a sufficient number of cases to retrieve the most similar case. We therefore require alternative arrangements. One such paradigm is rule-based reasoning RBR. In RBR, the knowledge of the scarcest resource, i.e., the domain experts, is codified in the form of IF-THEN rules and stored in the rule base.

Recall the early expert systems, which were classical rule-based systems utilized to emulate the decision-making ability of a human expert. Work in expert systems started in the early 1970s, when the most popular ones were developed, i.e., Prospector and MYCIN. The inference engine of a rule-based system works with deductive reasoning. If the antecedent of some rule matches the conditions at hand, then the consequent of that rule can be used to recommend a particular solution or action based on the domain problem. The major problem with these systems is what is called the knowledge-acquisition bottleneck. For this reason, CBR is used first and then RBR.

Knowledge Base

      Rule Base   // Rule Base is described by R $(R_1, R_2, R_3, ..., R_n)$

Input

      Feature Vector of the New Case $(NF_V = \{f_1, f_2, f_3, ..., f_f\})$

Output

      List of Actions (A_V)

RBR (NF_V)

For each rule R_i (0<=i<=n) in the Rule Base

      Compare NF_V with antecedent of the rule

      If antecedent of R_i matches with NF_V

            $A_V \leftarrow$ Fetch the consequent of R_i

If A_V null

      No expert advice available

6.6 Ongoing Case Study

Many classification and diagnosis problems fit this structure of reasoning, including diagnosing a microprocessor board, diagnosing a disease, and providing recommendations in an emergency. Let us discuss here the ongoing case study of an emergency.

6.6.1 Action Recommendation in Earthquake

Many researchers and authorities have developed systems for preparing for disasters and combating their effects. Various works include developing alert systems to provide SMS notifications, providing response plans, allocating and distributing resources (humanitarian aid, medicine, etc.), predicting future demands, and notifying affected people about safe places and available evacuation routes. Different web services, simulation tools, machine learning techniques, and reasoning approaches are utilized. Many emergency-response ontologies have been developed, including AccessOnto and SEMA4A. Major existing disaster-response systems send alert notifications for estimating resources, i.e., they respond only upon a request emerging from the disaster site. The ontology-supported hybrid reasoning framework integrates information in a common format coming from various heterogeneous sources, performs reasoning over it, and provides recommendations for resource estimation and timely allocation.

The input case is matched with existing cases based on the location of the incident, its severity, proximity, and availability of resources as and when information is updated from the disaster site. For example, in the case of an earthquake, the location feature (city, country) is readily available but not the magnitude; similarly, the number of casualties is an expensive feature. The objective of the base-filtering component is to retrieve all cases that match on the one free feature value, i.e., location.

References

Amailef, Khaled, and Jie Lu. "Ontology-supported case-based reasoning approach for intelligent m-Government emergency response services." *Decision Support Systems* 55, no. 1 (2013): 79–97.

Chakraborty, Baisakhi, Debashis Ghosh, Rahul Ranjan, Saswati Garnaik, and Narayan Debnath. "Knowledge management with case-based reasoning applied on fire emergency handling." In *2010 8th IEEE International Conference on Industrial Informatics*, pp. 708–713. IEEE 2010.

Haghighi, Pari Delir, Frada Burstein, Arkady Zaslavsky, and Paul Arbon. "Development and evaluation of ontology for intelligent decision support in medical emergency management for mass gatherings." *Decision Support Systems* 54, no. 2 (2013): 1192–1204.

Han, Yaoci, and Wei Xu. "An ontology-oriented decision support system for emergency management based on information fusion." In *Proceedings of the 1st ACM SIGSPATIAL International Workshop on the Use of GIS in Emergency Management*, pp. 1–8. Association for Computing Machinery, New York, NY, 2015.

Li, Xiang, Gang Liu, Anhong Ling, Jian Zhan, Ning An, Lian Li, and Yongzhong Sha. "Building a practical ontology for emergency response systems." In *2008 International Conference on Computer Science and Software Engineering*, Vol. 4, pp. 222–225. IEEE, 2008.

Malizia, Alessio, Teresa Onorati, Paloma Diaz, Ignacio Aedo, and Francisco Astorga-Paliza. "SEMA4A: an ontology for emergency notification systems accessibility." *Expert Systems with Applications* 37, no. 4 (2010): 3380–3391.

Masuwa-Morgan, Kristina R., and Phillip Burrell. "Justification of the need for an ontology for accessibility requirements (theoretic framework)." *Interacting with Computers* 16, no. 3 (2004): 523–555.

Onorati, Teresa, Alessio Malizia, Paloma Diaz, and Ignacio Aedo. "Modeling an ontology on accessible evacuation routes for emergencies." *Expert Systems with Applications* 41, no. 16 (2014): 7124–7134.

Papadopoulos, Homer, and Antonis Korakis. "Predicting medical resources required to be dispatched after earthquake and flood, using historical data and machine learning techniques: The COncORDE Emergency Medical Service use case." *International Journal of Interactive Communication Systems and Technologies* 8, no. 2 (2018): 13–35.

Qin, Yuchu, Wenlong Lu, Qunfen Qi, Xiaojun Liu, Meifa Huang, Paul J. Scott, and Xiangqian Jiang. "Towards an ontology-supported case-based reasoning approach for computer-aided tolerance specification." *Knowledge-Based Systems* 141 (2018): 129–147.

Rahaman, Saifur, and Mohammad Shahadat Hossain. "A belief rule based clinical decision support system to assess suspicion of heart failure from signs, symptoms and risk factors." In *2013 International Conference on Informatics, Electronics and Vision (ICIEV)*, pp. 1–6. IEEE, 2013.

Sahebjamnia, Navid, S. Ali Torabi, and S. Afshin Mansouri. "A hybrid decision support system for managing humanitarian relief chains." *Decision Support Systems* 95 (2017): 12–26.

Sehgal, Sukriti, Sahil Chaudhry, Prantik Biswas, and Sarika Jain. "A new genre of recommender systems based on modern paradigms of data filtering." *Procedia Computer Science* 92 (2016): 562–567.

Xu, Jinghai, Timothy L. Nyerges, and Gaozhong Nie. "Modeling and representation for earthquake emergency response knowledge: perspective for working with geo-ontology." *International Journal of Geographical Information Science* 28, no. 1 (2014): 185–205.

Zhang, Fushen, Shaobo Zhong, Simin Yao, Chaolin Wang, and Quanyi Huang. "Ontology-based representation of meteorological disaster system and its application in emergency management: illustration with a simulation case study of comprehensive risk assessment." *Kybernetes* 45, no. 5 (2016): 798–814.

Zhu, Min, Ruxue Chen, Shi Chen, Shaobo Zhong, Tianye Lin, and Quanyi Huang. "Ontology-supported case-based reasoning approach for double scenario model construction in international disaster medical relief action." In *International Conference on Applications and Techniques in Cyber Security and Intelligence ATCI 2018*, pp. 239–250. Springer, Cham, Switzerland, 2018.

7

Multilingual and Multimodal Access

Though semantic data models have become mainstream and gained popularity, they largely handle only textual data, and that only in English. Language-independent preservation of semantics and context related to a domain is required to attain equal status for all languages. Through this we can overcome national barriers which come from variations in languages. This will also facilitate cross-lingual access of information. This chapter discusses the motivation of multilingualism and multimodality and presents and exemplifies the ways through which they can be achieved in semantically enriched knowledge. Different use cases to access and manage this setup are also presented.

7.1 Motivation

The number of Internet users speaking a language other than English is increasing at a very fast pace. According to statistics from Internet World Stats (https://internetworldstats.com/stats7.htm), the number of Arabic-speaking Internet users in the world grew by 9348% in the last 20 years, followed by speakers of Russian (3653.40%). Figure 7.1 shows the growth for the six official languages of the United Nations—i.e., Arabic, English, French, Chinese, Spanish, and Russian—and some others. These are the languages spoken by the most Internet users, and about one-third of them are online at any given time. Although the number of English-speaking Internet users outranks even those who speak Chinese (the language with the most native speakers), the figure shows that growth among English speakers is not as quick as for other languages.

Despite the initial domination of the English language on the Internet, other languages are catching up very fast. The traditional web is by and large English based. Knowledge-representation strategies and data access and management strategies are English based. But today's generated data is largely multilingual, as is the current data web, where people of all

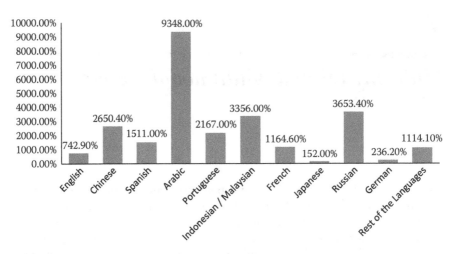

FIGURE 7.1
Growth of Internet Users by Language Spoken (2000–2020)

languages and cultures share and collaborate voluminously. This multi-lingual data published on the web can be exploited for better decision making. Language barriers must be overcome by providing cross-language access to ontologies. Semantic technologies can go a long way toward achieving the goal of removing the bias toward English language and culture, by tuning the semantic representation, storage, and inference mechanisms to multilingual and multicultural settings [Pretorius 2014, Jain et al. 2011].

When systems have language-independent representations, where they can present knowledge in the language of the user's choice, then we can say that we are utilizing the full potential of any product or service we humans have created—like the Internet. Imagine a scenario where a truly multilingual system can really make a difference: when a tourist is traveling to a country where he or she does not speak the native language. The tourist falls in urgent need of a medication but is unaware of the terminology used for those medicines in that country. Now imagine having a system that can take input in the user's native language or language of choice and provide seamless access to services with output in the user's language irrespective of the user's geographical location and the data required.

The aim is help people understand the communication in order to facilitate better decision making. In a broader sense, communication goes beyond linguistic resources. Multimodality is the interplay of different representations of data beyond just the text being multilingual. It describes practices involving spatial, visual, and aural resources to represent and communicate concepts.

7.1.1 Benefits of Multilingual and Multimodal Access

Systems which can accommodate information in multiple languages can facilitate the world in unprecedented ways. One of the most important benefits they present is allowing everyone to become a part of the twenty-first century's knowledge economy, since there will be no language barrier stopping non-English-speaking communities from joining. The publication, communication, biomedical, and tourism industries, among others, depend on a large number of textual data today. These industries can greatly benefit from other types of data as well—images, video, and audio—if provided. Multimodal representation facilitates policy decision making by disambiguating the understanding of concepts. Various ontologies are available in the bio-medical domain incorporating patient records, statistics, and information about diseases and symptoms. These ontologies must be translated into multiple languages for the internationalization of healthcare and incorporated with visual depictions of pathology test results. The Linked Open Data (LOD) Cloud allows organizations and individuals to present their existing data in a machine-understandable format [Berners-Lee 2009, Corlosquet et al. 2009]. LOD provides semantic interoperability for efficient management of data and information. Making this LOD Cloud multilingual and multimodal will provide better information and knowledge sharing, and hence better decision making and management.

7.2 Multilingual Knowledge Representation

In the last decade, researchers have started concentrating on the multilingual representation of information. The major problem encountered is that existing vocabularies are mostly in English. One option is to create an additional ontology for every language and every existing domain ontology. This is an unending, hard effort. Another option is to keep provisions for adding languages later, during the creation of the ontology. Three models exist in the literature for multilingual representation of ontologies [Espinoza et al. 2009].

7.2.1 Integration of Linguistic Constructs

This is the simplest of all the approaches, in which we incorporate multilingual information into the ontology itself. Various constructs of RDFS, SKOS, and OWL can be used for this, like rdfs:label, skos:prefLabel, skos:altLabel, and rdfs:comment. In this approach, interoperability is not an issue, as the linguistic information is stored in the ontology itself. The task of incorporating multilingual translation can be performed using like manual, automatic, or semi-automatic methods. In the manual way, the developer manually enters information in different languages into the ontology. In the automatic way, the ontology is passed through a system using tools like a translator to find translations, and then those translations are used to enrich the ontology. In the semi-automatic way, a human expert validates the automated translations before embedding them into the ontology.

Using this model, a multilingual ontology is constructed through two steps. The first step is creating an ontology in any (base) language. The translation in the required languages is incorporated using some OWL or RDFS construct. Let us exemplify it using a snippet from the "Animal" domain:

```
<owl:Class
rdf:about="http://www.semanticweb.org/vishal/ontologies/2018/10/
Indian_Biodiversity#Animal">
    <rdfs:subClassOf rdf:resource="http://www.semanticweb.org/vishal/
ontologies/2018/10/Indian_Biodiversity#Kingdom" />
    <owl:equivalentClass rdf:resource="http://www.semanticweb.org/vishal/
ontologies/2018/10/Indian_Biodiversity#जानवर"/>
    <owl:equivalentClassrdf:resource="http://www.semanticweb.org/vishal/
ontologies/2018/10/Indian_Biodiversity#पूराणी"/>
    <owl:equivalentClassrdf:resource="http://www.semanticweb.org/vishal/
ontologies/2018/10/Indian_Biodiversity#ਜਾਨਵਰ"/>
    <owl:equivalentClassrdf:resource="http://www.semanticweb.org/vishal/
ontologies/2018/10/Indian_Biodiversity#પશુ"/>
    <owl:equivalentClassrdf:resource="http://www.semanticweb.org/vishal/
ontologies/2018/10/Indian_Biodiversity#விலங்கீனக்கள்" />
<description xml:lang="en">The animal kingdom is the largest kingdom,
with over 1 million known species. All animals consist of many complex
cells. They are heterotrophs. Members of the animal kingdom are found in
the most diverse environments in the world.</description><description
xml:lang="hi">पशुसाम्राज्य1मलियिन से अधिक ज्ञात पुरजातियों के साथ सबसे बड़ा
साम्राज्य है। सभी जानवरों में कई जटलि कोशकिएं होती हैं। वे हेटरोट्रॉफ भी हैं। पशु
साम्राज्य के सदस्य दुनिया के सबसे वविधि वातावरण में पाए जाते हैं।</description>
<description xml:lang="mr">1दशल क्षपेक्षा अधिकि ज्ञात पुरजाती असलेले
पुराणी साम्राज्य सर्वात मोठे राज्य आहे. सर्व पुराण्यां मध्ये अनेक जटलि पेशी असतात.
तेदेखील हेटरोट्रॉफ आहेत. पुराणी साम्राज्या चे सदस्य जगातील वविधि पुरकारच्या
वातावरणात आढळतात.</description>
<description xml:lang="pa">ਜਾਨਵਰ ਦਾ ਰਾਜ 1 ਲੱਖ ਤੋਂ ਵੱਧ ਜਾਣੀਆ ਪੁਰਜਾਤੀਆਂ ਨਾਲ ਸਭ
ਤੋਂ ਵੱਡਾ ਰਾਜ ਹੈ. ਸਾਰੇ ਜਾਨਵਰ ਵਿੱਚ ਬਹੁਤ ਸਾਰੇ ਗੁੰਝਲਦਾਰ ਸੈੱਲ ਹੁੰਦੇ ਹਨ. ਉਹ ਵੀ ਹੈਟਰੋ ਟਰੋਫਸਹਨ. ਜਾਨਵਰ
ਦੇਸ ਦੱਸ ਦੁਨੀਆਂ ਦੇ ਸਭ ਤੋਂ ਵੱਧ ਵਭਿੰਨ ਮਾਹੋਲ ਵਿੱਚ ਮਲਿਦੇ ਹਨ।</description>
<description xml:lang="gu">પશુ સામ્રાજ્યઅે 10 મલિયિન જા ણીતી જાતઓિન
ੁ સૌથીમોਟੂਂਸਾਮ੍ਰਾਜ੍ਯਛੇ. બધા પૂਰਾਣੀ ઓમਾਂਧਣੁ ਜਟਵਿਕੋਸ਼ਕਿਓ ਹੋਯ ਛੇ. ਤੇઓਹੇਟਿਰੋਟ੍ਰੋੂਫ਼ਸਪਣੁਛੇ.
ਪੂਰਾਣੀਸਾਮੂਰਾਜ੍ਯਨਾਸਭ੍ਯੋਵਸ਼੍ਿਵਨਾਸੌਥੀਵੇਵਧ੍ਿਯਸਭਰਪਰ੍ਯਾਵਰਣੋਮਾਂਜੋਵਾਮਗੋਲੇਛੇ.</description>
<description xml:lang="ta">விலங் கஇிராச்சி யம்1 மி ல்லீ யனாஈக்ஈம்அதீ
கமானஉ யிரினானஈகள்ஈஒ·ரண்டமிகப்பெரியஇிராச் சியம்ஆகஈம். அனை த்தூ
```

वी லங்கஙகளைாம்பலசிக் கலானசெல்கள்உள்ளன. அ வர்கள் ஹெட்ட்டே·ராே·ர ட்ர ெஂப் கள். வி லங் குஇரா ச்சி யத்தி ன்உ றுப்பி னர் கள்உ ல கில் மிக வாம் வேரேொபட்டசஂழல்களில்காணப்படஂகின்றனர்.</description>

```
<rdfs:label xml:lang="en">Animal</rdfs:label>
<rdfs:label xml:lang="hi">जानवर</rdfs:label>
<rdfs:label xml:lang="mr">पुराणी</rdfs:label>
<rdfs:label xml:lang="pa">ਜਾਨਵਰ</rdfs:label>
<rdfs:label xml:lang="gu">પશુ</rdfs:label>
<rdfs:label xml:lang="ta">விலங்கஂகள்</rdfs:label>
</owl:Class>
```

This example represents multilingual information using xml:lang for the concept "Animal." For the name of the concept in different languages, rdfs:label is used; and description (an annotation property) is used to provide description. Figure 7.2 is a screenshot of the Protégé tree view.

7.2.2 Ontology Mediation

In this approach, every conceptualization is stored in a different ontology and then mediated, which is the process of reconciling the differences between two

FIGURE 7.2
Integrating Linguistic Constructs

ontologies. Using this model, the multilingual ontology is constructed through two steps. The first step is looking for or creating the same domain ontology in all the required languages by following the methodology in Section 4.1. All these ontologies are then mapped for similarities in the next step. Domain-related terms in different vocabularies are joined or mapped to establish a common semantic relationship. The classes are related using owl:equivalentClass property; for instances, owl:sameAs is used. Figure 7.3 shows the connections established between similar terms in different languages.

Following are ontologies for "person" in English and Hindi and the mapping between corresponding classes in English, Hindi, and Portuguese.

```
##### ###### ###### ###### ###### ###### ###### ###### ###### ##########
#                        Ontology in English                #
##### ###### ###### ###### ###### ###### ###### ###### ###### ##########
```
:Personrdf:typeowl:class; rdfs:label "person"@en;
rdfs:comment "A person is a being that has certain capacities or attributes, such as reason, morality, consciousness or self-consciousness, and is a part of a culturally established form of social relations such as kinship, owner-ship of property, or legal responsibility."@en. :Malerdf:type owl:Class;
  rdfs:label "Male"@en;
  rdfs:comment "Male carries XY chromosomes."@en;
  rdfs:subClassOf:Person. :Femalerdf:type owl:Class;
  rdfs:label "Female";
  rdfs:comment "Female carries XX chromosomes.";
  rdfs:subClassof:Person. :Sisterrdf:type owl:Class;
  rdfs:label "Sister";
  rdfs:comment "A Female Sibling. ";
  rdfs:subClassof:Female.
```
##### ###### ###### ###### ###### ###### ###### ###### ###### ##########
#                        Ontology in Hindi                  #
##### ###### ###### ###### ###### ###### ###### ###### ###### ##########
```
:व्यक्तिrdf:type owl:Class; rdfs:label "व्यक्ति"@hi;

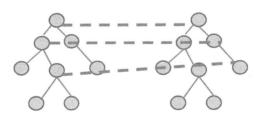

FIGURE 7.3
Ontology Mediation

rdfs:comment"एक व्यक्ति एक ऐसा व्यक्ति होता है जसिमें कुछ क्षमताएं या गुण होते हैं जैसे कारण, नेतिकिता, चेतनाया आत्म-चेतना,औरसांस्कृतिकिरूपसेस्थापतिसामाजकिसंबंधों का एक हसिसाब नना जैसे रशि्तेदारी, सम्पतिका स्वामति्वयाक़ानूनी जमि्मेदारी।" @hi.
:पुरुषrdf:type owl:Class;
   rdfs:label "पुरुष"@hi;
   rdfs:comment "पुरुषमेंएक्सवाईगुणसूत्रहैं।"@hi;
   rdfs:subClassof:व्यक्ति. :महलिाrdf:type owl:Class;
   rdfs:label "महलिा"@hi;
   rdfs:comment "महलिामेंएक्सएक्सगुणसूत्रहैं।"@hi;
   rdfs:subClassof:व्यक्ति. :बहनrdf:type owl:Class;
   rdfs:label "बहन"@hi;
   rdfs:comment "एकबहनमहलिाभाईहैं।"@hi;
   rdfs:subClassof:महलिा.

```
##### ###### ###### ###### ###### ###### ###### ###### ###### ###########
#          Mapping corresponding classes in different languages       #
##### ###### ###### ###### ###### ###### ###### ###### ###### ###########
```

@prefix:<http://www.semanticweb.org/vishal/ontologies/2017/12/PersonOntology#>.
@prefix owl:<http://www.w3.org/2002/07/owl#>.
@prefix rdf:<http://www.w3.org/1999/02/22-rdf-sytax-ns#>.
@prefix xml:<http://www.w3.org/XML/1998/namespace>.
@prefix xsd:<http://www.w3.org/2001/XMLSchema#>.
@prefix rdfs:<http://www.w3.org/2000/01/rdf-schema#>.
@base<http://www.semanticweb.org/vishal/ontologies/2017/12/PersonOntology>.
<http://www.semanticweb.org/vishal/ontologies/2017/12/PersonOntology>
rdf:typeowl:Ontology;:versionInfo"v.1.5."@en:Personowl:equivalentClass:व्यक्ति;
owl:equivalentClass:Pessoa. :Maleowl:equivalentClass:पुरुष;
owl:equivalentClass:Masculino. :Femaleowl:equivalentClass:महलिा;
owl:equivalentClass:Femea. :Sisterowl:equivalentClass:बहन;
owl:equivalentClass:Irma.

After these steps, we can access the information in multiple languages (in the languages where ontologies are present). Through this we aim to achieve interoperability between multiple ontologies concerning the same domain but in different languages.

7.2.3 Globalization

In the language context, globalization is an approach that aims to address and give equal status to all languages. It incorporates internationalization and localization to accomplish the goal of multilingualism. Its basic principle is as follows:

$$Globalization = Internationalization + n*Localization$$

Globalization describes the comprehensive process that takes into account language translation and cultural integration (aka internationalization and localization). Internationalization (I18N) is the planning and implementation of products and services so that they can be easily be localized for specific languages.

In this approach we try to make ontologies linguistically rich while keeping the information morphosyntactically correct. Here the efforts of the ontology engineer are saved because we are using already-available ontologies to define the concepts. This model concentrates on the separation of implementation details from linguistic resources. Linguistic resources are available as multilingual dictionaries, corpora, lexicons, terminologies, and thesauruses. This approach standardizes the ontology development process, allowing the developer to use variables instead of language-specific texts, which in turn makes for a dynamic knowledge base. This process of creating ontologies is called internationalization (I18n). Then the ontology can be localized very easily to any language of choice, called localization (L10n).

There are multiple multilingual repositories of ontologies available from which we can associate linguistic information into the ontology, or we can make our own. Following are some of those repositories:

- **WordNet:** WordNet is a lexical database and can be considered an electronic dictionary. It contains nouns, verbs, adverbs, and adjectives along with idioms and simplex words.
- **DBpedia:** DBpedia is an effort at extracting all the structured information of Wikipedia, representing it semantically in the form of RDF triples, and making it available on the semantic web.
- **BabelNet:** BabelNet is a very large, wide-coverage multilingual semantic network. It is a resource which is constructed automatically through integration of knowledge from WordNet and Wikipedia. Along with this machine learning, translations are used to enrich the repository with lexical multilingual information.
- **YAGO:** YAGO is a combination of Wikipedia, WordNet, GeoNames, and more.

Figure 7.4 shows a part of the LOD Cloud diagram. We can see how everything on the web can be connected together and can provide information of unprecedented scale, in which if we look for anything, the result will contain all the available information related to that concept.

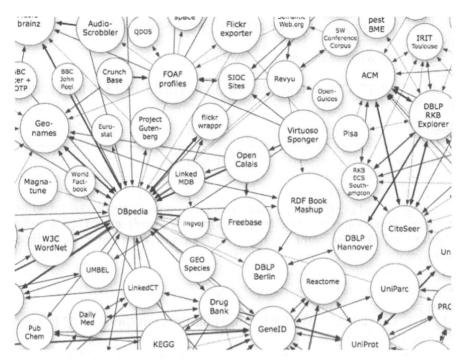

FIGURE 7.4
LOD Cloud (*Source:* linkeddata.org)

7.3 Multilingual Keyword Search

This form of search finds knowledge associated with the textual data. The keyword could be a domain-related concept, property, instance of the concept, or literal value of the instance. When the keyword is passed as an input, a SPARQL query is generated which gathers and presents all the semantically associated information as an output. In addition to this, the language in which the keyword is entered is also the language of the result.

7.3.1 Demonstration of Multilingual Search in Hindi

Language in which result is to be displayed: Hindi
    PREFIX rdf: <http://www.w3.org/1999/02/22-rdf-syntax-ns#>
    PREFIX owl: <http://www.w3.org/2002/07/owl#>
    PREFIX rdfs: <http://www.w3.org/2000/01/rdf-schema#>
    PREFIX xsd: <http://www.w3.org/2001/XMLSchema#>

PREFIX ns: <http://www.semanticweb.org/vishal/ontologies/2018/10/ Indian_Biodiversity#>
Enter the keyword to be searched: Animal
Query:
  SELECT DISTINCT * WHERE {ns:Animal?Property?Info. FILTER langMatches (lang(?Info),"hi")}

Result:

Property	Info
===	===
rdfs:label	"जानवर"@hi
<http://purl.org/dc/elements/1.1#description>	"पशुसाम्राज्य 1 मलियिन से अधिक ज्ञात परजातियों के साथ सबसे बड़ा साम्राज्य है। सभी जानवरों में कई जटलि कोशकिाएं होती हैं। वे हेटरोट्रॉफ भी हैं। पशु साम्राज्य के सदस्य दुनयिा के सबसे वविधि वातावरण में पाए जाते हैं।" @hi

---

Enter the keyword to be searched: Fungi
Query:
SELECT DISTINCT * WHERE { ns:Fungi?Property?Info. FILTER lang Matches(lang(?Info),"hi")}

Property	Info
===	===
rdfs:label	"कवक"@hi
<http://purl.org/dc/elements/1.1#description>	"मशरूम, मोल्ड और फफूंदी कवक के राज्य में सभी जीवहैं। अधकिांश कवक बहु कोशकिीय होते हैं और इसमें कई जटलि कोशकिाएं होती हैं। कुछ कवक स्वाद महान और दूसरों को मार सकते हैं! फंगीजी व हैं जो जीव वज्ञिानी एक बार पौधों से उलझन में हैं, हालांकि, पौधों के वपिरीत, कवक अपना खाना नहीं बना सकते हैं।अधकिांश अपने भोजन को पौधों के कुछ हस्सिों से बनाते हैं जो मट्टिी में क्षय हो रहे हैं।"@hi

---

7.3.2 Demonstration of Multilingual Search in Punjabi

Language in which result is to be displayed: Punjabi
  PREFIX rdf: <http://www.w3.org/1999/02/22-rdf-syntax-ns#>
  PREFIX owl: <http://www.w3.org/2002/07/owl#>
  PREFIX rdfs: <http://www.w3.org/2000/01/rdf-schema#>
  PREFIX xsd: <http://www.w3.org/2001/XMLSchema#>
  PREFIX ns: <http://www.semanticweb.org/vishal/ontologies/2018/10/ Indian_Biodiversity#>
Enter the keyword to be searched: Animal
Query:

```
SELECT DISTINCT * WHERE { ns:Animal?Property?Info. FILTER
langMatches(lang(?Info),"pa")}
```

| Property | Info
==
  |rdfs:label | "ਜਾਨਵਰ"@pa
  |<http://purl.org/dc/elements/1.1#description>| "ਜਾਨਵ ਰਦਾਰਾਜ1ਲੱਖ ਤੋਵੱਧ
ਜਾਣਿਆਪੁਰ ਜਾਤੀਆਂਨਾ ਲਸਭਤੋਵੱਡਾਰਾ ਜਹੈ. ਸਾਰੇ ਜਾਨ ਵਰਵੀਂ ਚਬਹੁ ਤਸਾਰੇਗੁੱਝਲਦਾਰਸੈੱਲਹੁੰਦੇਹਨ.
ਉਹਵੀਹੈਟਰੋਟਰੋਫਸਹਨ. ਜਾਨਵਰਦੇਸਦੱਸਦੂਨੀਆਂਦੇਸਭਤੋਵੱਧਵਿਭਿਨਿਮਾਹੌਲਵਿੱਚਮਿਲਦੇਹਨ।"@pa |

Query:
```
SELECT DISTINCT * WHERE {ns:Fungi?Property?Info. FILTER
langMatches(lang(?Info),"pa")}
```

| Property | Info
==
  |rdfs:label | "ਫੰਜਾਈ"@pa
  |<http://purl.org/dc/elements/1.1#description>| "ਫੰਜਾਈਦੇਰਾਜਵਿੱਚਮਸ਼ਰੂਮਜ਼,
ਉੱਲੀਅਤੇਫ਼ਫੂੰਦੀਸਾਰੇਜੀਵਹੁੰਦੇਹਨ. ਜ਼ਿਆਦਾਤਰ ਫੰਜਾਈ ਮਲਟੀਸੈਲ_ਲਰਹੁੰਦੇਹਨਅ ਤੇਬਹੁਤਸਾਰੇਗੁੱਝਲ ਦਾਰ
ਸੈੱਲਹੁੰਦੇਹਨ. ਕੁੱਝਫੰਜੀਆਂਦਾਸਵਾਗਤਕਰਦਾਹੈਅਤੇਦੂਸਰੇਤੁਹਾਨੂੰਮਾਰਸਕਦੇਹਨ! ਫੰਗੀਉਹਜੀਵਹਨਜੋਜੀਵ- ਜੰਤੂਆ
ਨੂੰਪਲਾਂਟਾਂਨਾਲਇਕਕਵਾਰਉਲਝਣਵਿਚਲਿਆਉਦੇਸਨ, ਹਲਾਂਕਿ, ਪੌਦਿਆਂਤੋਉਲਟ, ਫੰਜਾਈਆ ਪਟਾਭੋਜ ਨਨਹੀਬ
ਝਾਸਕ ਦੇਜ਼ਿਆਦਾਤਰਉਨ੍ਹਾਂਪੌਦਿਆਂਦੇਖਾਣੇਤੋਭੋਜਨਬਣਾਉਂਦੇਹਨਜੋਮੈਟੀਵਿਚਿਨਸ਼ਟਹੋਜਾਂਦੇਹਨ."@pa |

```

On a search of a language- specific concept or term, the module searches
through the ontology and results for all concept-related knowledge. The
SPARQL query is generated on the basis of the chosen language and key-
word to carry out the retrieval accordingly.

---

## 7.4 Multimedia Semantic Integration and Resource Access

Multimodal basically means knowledge modeled in different forms, be it
textual, multimedia, images, video, etc. Media provides a perceptual de-
scription as compared to a conceptual (text- only) description. A huge
number and variety of multimedia metadata models exist with different
goals, scopes, and levels of detail. The problem is in interoperating these
models and making them semantically unambiguous. The Multimedia
Content Description Interface (MPEG-7) and MPEG-21 multimedia frame-
work are two such standards for describing multimedia content. Ontologies
have proven to be an interoperable and unambiguous way of representing
semantics, along with the reasoning support. Ontologies can be utilized for
```

perceptual modeling. Today, many multimedia vocabularies exist on the semantic web, but the semantic gap in multimedia is still a research question. This section exemplifies a multimedia ontology utilizing Multimedia Web Ontology Language (MOWL), an extended multimedia version of OWL.

7.4.1 Multimedia Ontology Construction

For drafting a multimedia ontology, a handcrafted text file is to be written using MOWL along with the basic building constructs of RDF, RDFS, and OWL. In order to carry out integration of multimedia content, <mowl:Concept> has been used, which manifests the real-world entity or instance or concept, and <mowl:hasMediaExample> and <mowl:MediaExample> to embed the concept- and media-related properties. The domain of disaster management has been taken for demonstration purposes. Following is a snippet of a MOWL text file showing that multimedia content like an image is associated using the MOWL property <mowl:hasMediaExample> and corresponding media content is embedded using <mowl:MediaExample>:

```
<owl:Classrdf:ID="Event">
<rdfs:subClassOf rdf:resource="&mowl;Concept"/>
</owl:Class>
<owl:Classrdf:ID= "DisasterManagement">
<rdfs:subClassOf rdf:resource="#Event"/>
<mowl:hasMediaExample rdf:resource="#DM"/>
</owl:Class>
<owl:Classrdf:ID="EmergencySituation">
<rdfs:subClassOf rdf:resource="&mowl;Concept"/>
</owl:Class>
<owl:Classrdf:ID="EmergencyResponse">
<rdfs:subClassOf rdf:resource="#Requirements"/>
</owl:Class>
<owl:ObjectProperty rdf:ID="callsForAn">
<rdfs:domain rdf:resource="Disaster"/>
<rdfs:range rdf:resource="EmergencySituation"/>
</owl:ObjectProperty>
<owl:ObjectProperty rdf:ID="callsFor">
<rdfs:domain nrdf:resource="DisasterManagement"/>
<rdfs:range rdf:resource="EmergencySituation"/>
</owl:ObjectProperty>
<mowl:MediaExample rdf:ID="DM">
<mowl:hasURI>C:\Users\VISHAL\NIT\MediaExamples\DM2.jpg</
mowl:hasURI>
</mowl:MediaExample>
```

7.4.2 Multimedia Visualization

Visualization of a multimedia ontology follows a series of steps. First, the MOWL parser is required to parse the domain ontology and deploy it into a Bayesian network. To carry out that process, we require APIs like NanoXML (a non-validating parser for Java) and Netica-J, which provides support to the Bayesian network. Netica-J is used to represent relationships between concepts even in the presence of uncertainty. Parsing of the disaster multimedia ontology results in a .dot file that contains its generated Bayesian network. This .dot file is fed into a tool like GVedit (from Graphviz) to decode it into an image.

7.4.3 Multimedia Search

In searching for any multimedia content for a concept, here "Fungi," the corresponding SPARQL query gives the path to the multimedia content, i.e., image:

```
Enter the keyword to be searched: Fungi
PREFIX rdf: <http://www.w3.org/1999/02/22-rdf-syntax-ns#>
PREFIX owl: <http://www.w3.org/2002/07/owl#>
PREFIX rdfs: <http://www.w3.org/2000/01/rdf-schema#>
PREFIX xsd: <http://www.w3.org/2001/XMLSchema#>
PREFIX ns: <http://www.semanticweb.org/vishal/ontologies/2018/10/
Indian_Biodiversity#>
SELECT?ImagePath {?X rdf:typens:Fungi.?X ns:hasImage?ImagePath }
```

```
| ImagePath |
```
==
```
| "/home/abs/Documents/Files/BrowseJAIV/Images/fungi.jpg"^^xsd:-
string |
```

References

Berners-Lee, Tim. Linked Data-Design Issues. World Wide Web Consortium, 2009. Available at https://www.w3.org/DesignIssues/LinkedData.html (last accessed on 01.08.2020).

Corlosquet, Stéphane, Renaud Delbru, Tim Clark, Axel Polleres, and Stefan Decker. "Produce and consume linked data with Drupal!" In *The Semantic Web—ISWC 2009*, pp. 763–778. Springer, Berlin, Germany, 2009.

Espinoza, Mauricio, Elena Montiel- Ponsoda, and Asunción Gómez-Pérez. "Ontology localization." In *Proceedings of the Fifth International Conference on Knowledge Capture*, pp. 33–40. Association for Computing Machinery, New York, NY, 2009.

Jain, Sarika, Deepa Chaudhary, and N. K. Jain. "Localization of EHCPRs system in the multilingual domain: an implementation." In *Information Systems for Indian Languages: ICISIL 20011*, pp. 314–316. Springer, Berlin, Germany, 2011.

Pretorius, Laurette. "The multilingual semantic web as virtual knowledge commons: the case of the under-resourced South African languages." In *Towards the Multilingual Semantic Web*, pp. 49–66. Springer, Berlin, Germany, 2014.

8

Concluding Remarks and Outlook for the Future

The flood of data in all disciplines and domains poses a critical challenge to every organization that is attempting to derive and demonstrate value from its massive and rich variety of data sources and digital resources. The challenge is manifest in several areas: data discovery, data access, analytic modeling, and the three Rs of knowledge discovery—representation, recall, and re-purposing. Semantic AI technologies enable smarter data analytics, empower more actionable intelligence, and equip diverse participants in the modern knowledge workplace. Semantic AI is the foundation of the right AI: accelerated, actionable, adaptable, amplified, and augmented intelligence.

Emergency response decisions are complex because of the extraordinary demands that disaster events present to a team. Unconventional emergencies are dynamic and unpredictable situations involving multiple geospatial requirements, different organizations, personnel, unassessed risks, and legal issues. Semantic intelligence has come to the rescue.

This book is an attempt to integrate the full potential of existing approaches, tools, techniques, and methodologies to provide situation awareness and advisory support to end-users in a seamless manner. As discussed in Chapter 2, semantic technologies serve as an enabler for collecting and fusing heterogeneous and unstructured information from various sources and integrating it to provide situation awareness and hence facilitate decision making during catastrophic disasters. The semantic intelligence of machines aids them in understanding inconsistent information originating from different sources. The first step toward achieving this goal is using the semantic data model RDF, the second is making data accessible via queries, and the third is making the implicit data explicit via inference. This is possible because of the data integration and interoperability provided by semantic technologies and machine-understandable representation structures, facilitating follow-up on decisions.

Semantic technologies are ever-evolving, but today a point has been reached where many of them are well established and stable. This book has presented the prototypical development of a semantically intelligent system to demonstrate the applicability of semantic technologies. Ontological knowledge bases have been created for both earthquakes and terrorism as sample unconventional emergencies. The simulated environment provides use cases for resource management and advisory support. The complete selected knowledge base can be browsed, navigated, queried, and searched for keyword descriptions. The advisory module provides advice for decision making by the semantic technologies.

Semantic technologies as utilized for a prototypical solution off-line can similarly be utilized to develop online web portals. In the long run, the developed portal can allow data to be fed in real time, thereby affecting the recommendations. The domain ontology, domain case base, and domain rule base for other emergencies can be prepared with the procedural knowledge remaining the same. The knowledge representation model can be adjusted to a multilingual setting using any of the three approaches discussed in Chapter 7. In addition to SPARQL, the user may be allowed to query in natural language and not restricted to only predefined queries.

Index